Why I Left
Jehovah's Witnesses

OF THIS ONE THING I AM MOST DETERMINED:
TO MAKE MY CALLING AND ELECTION SURE.

2 Peter 1:10

Why I Left Jehovah's Witnesses

Ted Dencher

Foreword by
PAUL B. SMITH, B.A., D.D., F.R.G.S.

LAKELAND
MARSHALL MORGAN & SCOTT
116 Baker Street
London W1M 2BB

First Impression 1966
Second Impression 1968
Third Impression 1969
Fourth Impression 1970
Fifth Impression 1972
Sixth Impression 1973
Seventh Impression 1975

ISBN 0 551 00443 6

Printed in Great Britain by
Hunt Barnard Printing Ltd, Aylesbury, Bucks.

Foreword

Every four years I bring a series of messages on the various false teachers of this generation. My series generally commences with Jehovah's Witnesses and concludes with the Unitarians. Along with most pastors, I welcome every new work on these subjects and Ted Dencher's personal testimony will undoubtedly prove to be of great value to those pastors across the world who are constantly looking for new material on this rapidly growing sect.

Mr. Dencher has preached in the pulpit of The Peoples Church in Toronto, Canada and his messages have proved most effective. His preaching is extremely practical and based almost entirely upon his intimate knowledge of these people and his study in depths of the Word of God.

Why I Left Jehovah's Witnesses will be added to my library on the subject and used with great profit and spiritual blessing among our people.

P.B.S.

Contents

Introduction

It is with deep gratitude to my risen Lord and Saviour that I set forth this book to the public. Through the Holy Spirit, who first convicted me of my sin, I found repentance and afterward conversion. From repentance I turned to the Saviour who, upon the cross, gave Himself as an atonement for me. Turning to Him I found salvation, and was thus united to God the Father.

My prayer is that others, who do not know Him as I have come to know Him, shall come to be His children. If those who have never been truly redeemed could only realize what they are missing, and will miss throughout eternity, they would wait no longer, but would turn to Him and be saved. It is not within my power to do anything primary towards the salvation of another. I can only tell of my experience with God and relate what the Scriptures reveal as to how others can come unto Him. The rest is up to God and the person involved.

Various individuals view me with mixed feelings. Some wonder, for instance, why I am in the full-time itinerant ministry. Others wonder why I have even written a book. Still others pass me off as someone with a gripe against Jehovah's Witnesses. Generally, I find that those with a severe critical or questioning attitude towards any prominent servant of God are usually unaware of the true depth of spiritual experience it is possible to attain through salvation. They apply their own feelings to others. This causes them to react in various ways. Yet there are others who fully realize what is behind it all. It is to those that this book is especially dedicated.

I am trying to bring Jehovah's Witnesses and Christians together. Why so? For the purpose of having Jehovah's Witnesses hear the gospel of salvation through Christ. Something has put a wedge between these Witnesses and the Christians. This must be removed. Hatred has proved to be the biggest factor in this separation. Love can win over and replace hatred successfully. It is towards this goal that I strive.

Jehovah's Witnesses do not realize that I have their best interests in mind. They imagine that I am against them. Yet if I were, I would make no effort whatsoever towards their finding eternal life with our Lord. I would not care to what destiny their souls departed at death. I would leave them to face this alone, and then laugh at their poor, pitiful condition.

Naturally, the Witnesses do not appreciate efforts made on their behalf. They feel no lack of anything. This makes their condition all the more serious. Having been one of them, I know how they think and how they feel towards others. I can sympathize with them. I am their friend in the church. It is my prayer that they all shall someday stand in the image of the Saviour, forgiven and redeemed forevermore.

Many of these Witnesses were dear friends of mine for many years. My heart is exceedingly sad when I think of the heaven they might miss. It is sometimes more than I can bear, and therefore I commit them in prayer to God. If only there were something in my power to transform them into God's children, born anew! What little has been entrusted me, however, I shall continue to perform and hold forth while I have breath.

I am only one person, and can only do so much. But there are many thousands of you Christians, scattered throughout the many denominations of our churches in many countries. Do you love the Christ who bought you? Would you do Him a service? Then forget not my former brethren; do not pass them by. They are people just like yourselves. They have hearts and minds, consciences and souls; and above all, a Saviour who died to redeem them.

It grieves me to hear of the mis-treatment many Witnesses receive from your hands. How would Jesus treat you, if you were to knock on His door? How would you yourself like to be treated if knocking upon the door of another? *That* is the way you should be treating Jehovah's Witnesses! Or have you forgotten the elementary, beginning rule of the Christian faith—to do unto others as you would have them do unto you? How can you mistreat a person for whom Jesus died? He died for them no less than He died for you. Do you cause

10

Jehovah's Witnesses to realize *that* whenever they meet you?

Is there any real difference between you and the non-Christians that Jehovah's Witnesses meet everywhere they go? If so, what is that difference? Does the love of God flow through you? Do they detect the longing and yearning in your heart to see them come to Christ? Would you shed tears in prayer on their behalf? Would you preach unendingly to make known the riches of salvation through Christ on their behalf? Exactly what *does* a Jehovah's Witness detect about you that he does not see in others who are *not* Christians?

You see, it is not only a readiness on the part of the Jehovah's Witness to hear the word of God that is needed; it is also your *preparedness to give* that word.

Prepared both by study and an undergirding of the Holy Spirit, fortified by fervent prayer. If Jehovah's Witnesses continue to meet *prepared* Christians as they go from house to house, they will come face to face with Jesus Christ, and be forced to come to a decision as to what they personally think of Him.

Christians, lay down your swords! Not only against Jehovah's Witnesses (and all others who are not true Christians), but against each other! Lay hold upon the true fight, which is not against flesh and blood. Your fight is a spiritual one, and you cannot fight this fight alone. God will go before you if you will but call upon Him. Let us more and more seek the unity the Spirit will give us as we unitedly preach the risen Lord and Saviour of our lives.

Let us concern ourselves with that which matters most. There are many problems that have been with us and will remain after we are gone—unsolved by us. Let us not get sidetracked into something that does not glorify and exemplify the Saviour. Otherwise we lose the effectiveness of our message.

I am proud to be a part of the church universal, the body of Jesus Christ. It is my desire to implement it until He comes. It is my sincere prayer that I shall build, and not destroy; uphold, not tear down; fortify, not cause to disintegrate. May I always encourage love, discourage hatred. Yes, let us ever be one, brethren, even as we someday shall be one, united evermore within the realms of His heavenly glory.

1

How And Why I Became
A Jehovah's Witness

I SEARCH FOR GOD

Attempting to find God and find His people is no easy task. So I discovered in 1945. Our country had just come through World War II, and I was out of school and working. I had made a vow to myself that someday I would find God and unite with His people. Toward that end I started searching.

Having had no Bible training or Christian education, I was at a loss as to what to do. I have always been deeply touched by music—and I began to accompany myself on the guitar and express myself in song. As a child I played the mandolin and ukulele. I learned some of the profound truths of the Scriptures through the Negro spirituals. They were always telling of what God had done and was yet to do. I learned that Christ was to return and cleave the sky with His presence; then open the graves for the dead to come forth.

I began to wonder: What do *I* do in order to experience all of this favourably? Would I ever be ready to face death? What about the great judgment? Where would *I* stand? Could I stand my trial all alone? When Jesus came, would He come for *me*? Those questions began to haunt me, with no apparent source of answers at hand.

One thing I began to cultivate: An awe and reverence for God and a desire to read and understand the Bible. And so I attempted to do just that. What an impossible task it seemed to be! Where did one begin reading the Bible? Did you start at the first book and read through to the finish, like any other book? I tried that and did not seem to be getting what I wanted. Yet the beauty and uniqueness of this Book held me. I could not let it go. How I longed to understand it! How

I longed to find God and be reconciled to Him! But there was no one to show me the way to Him.

Around 1942, at our home in Jenkintown, Pennsylvania, I had accepted some literature from a Jehovah's Witness who came to our door. But I had read in the book that was left with me (*The New World*) that they did not believe in hell as a literal place of conscious punishment for the unrepentent wicked, and I could see that the Bible clearly taught otherwise. And so I put the literature aside and did not read any further. Needless to say, no Christian had come to my home to speak with me about these things. No Christian has come since then, and I suppose no Christian ever will! And so I was left to try and find the answers all by myself. Naturally I did not find them!

Then, in 1946, I read an article in *The Reader's Digest* magazine; it was called "Peddlers of Paradise", and was about Jehovah's Witnesses. It described a strange cult that seemed to be persecuted by American mobs for their faith! It described how they were attacked by mobs for refusing to salute the flag! Well now! *Here* was something decidedly *different*! This bears investigation!

I remembered that I had accepted literature from them just a few years back. We still had the literature in the house (we had now moved to Philadelphia). I found it and began to read it. Why, it wasn't as bad as I thought! *The Watchtower* magazine told that we were now free from the law and did not have to keep the ten commandments! That was reassuring to me! I had tried to keep those commandments and failed, of course. *The Watchtower* said that we could still find favour with God. *That* is what *I* had been trying to discover! —how? I read the article through and then read the bound book. I was convinced: this deserved prompt investigation!

I decided to write to the Watch Tower Society for a subscription to *The Watchtower* magazine. Before the magazine started coming, two young men came to my house and said they were Jehovah's Witnesses. I could see they did not believe in a mail order religion! The Society had notified the local congregation (then called *company*), and they in turn had sent two full-time workers to see me.

These men sat down and talked with me, and suggested that they would be glad to hold a Bible study with me once a week, at whatever time I selected! They had come to the

14

right house! They also invited me to the Kingdom Hall. I did not take them up on *that* right away, but I permitted them to come and study with me.

ENTER JEHOVAH'S WITNESSES

We began to study a book titled *The Kingdom Is At Hand*. The Watch Tower Society, I learned, was holding an international convention in Cleveland, Ohio, that summer (1946). I decided I would attend. I did and was much impressed by what I saw and heard. I had by that time started attending meetings at the Kingdom Hall. It all seemed wonderful to me. I felt that I had finally hit upon what I had been searching for. The study in our home continued, and I became a regular attender at all Kingdom Hall and area study meetings. It was not long until they had talked me into joining the *theocratic ministry school* (which it isn't; in reality it is a speech class). This is held on the same evening as the *service meeting* (at which sales and business procedures are discussed). In the "ministry school" one learns to give talks before an audience, and in that manner my public speaking career began. From this class one usually enters the next phase—going from door to door.

I FACE THE PUBLIC

After I had been attending meetings regularly for a couple months, a Witness friend suggested I accompany him from door to door to see how the work is done. Having talked me into it, I agreed to go. There I saw that people *could* talk about the controversial subject of religion to total strangers and get away with it! Soon I was going from house to house by myself. Gaining confidence, I began to pursue such activity every weekend.

Then there was the street work: We would hand out handbills advertising the public lecture given at Kingdom Hall on Sundays. It was customary to wear "sandwich" signs in this work. Also, we offered the magazines *Consolation* (since become *Awake!*) and *The Watchtower* to passers-by.

By now I had been sold solidly on the organization, and I decided to be baptized. They baptize by total immersion. And so, in January of 1947, I was baptized at a local "circuit assembly". Now I was considered an *ordained minister*!

I BEGIN A "WATCHTOWER MINISTRY"

Now at this point I must go back a little, and point out some facts. As soon as I made acquaintances in the organization, I was struck by the manner in which they told others what to do. The current "party line" when I came in was "don't get married—Armageddon is right around the corner!" It seemed that marriage might somehow cramp one's style, or spoil his chances of getting through Armageddon alive. Just exactly how, they never explained. At any rate, they frowned upon marriage. The same with education. Also upon anything else worthwhile.

Remember my interest in music? Although at the age of sixteen I had mashed my left hand in an accident at work, I came through all right, and decided I would like to learn to play the guitar professionally and make a living playing and singing the music I love. Jehovah's Witnesses soon put a damper on *that* idea! They frown upon any individual effort of a person to make something of himself. They discourage ambition *in totc*—except, of course, the works you perform for the organization! You had to sell yourself out to the organization completely, or not at all. So although I continued playing for my own enjoyment (plus some radio and stage work), I was forced by the pressure of the organization eventually to put aside all interests in this, and sell out to the Watch Tower Society.

And so I had to permit my natural talents to lie idle, because the Watch Tower demanded all or nothing. Since I was convinced that *this* was *God's* organization, I set aside my personal interests and gave it to the organization.

By going from house to house, giving speeches from the Kingdom Hall platform, attending the meetings and conventions, I was considered a *minister*. And I, of course, believed that I was one. I could not believe otherwise. And this now leads into my next subject:

HOW I WAS CONVINCED TO BECOME A J.W.

So far I have not mentioned the doctrines—what I was told

I must believe as a Jehovah's Witness. What I know now and what I knew then are, of course, two different things. But now I want to tell you exactly what struck me as being unique about the organization, and what led me to finally conclude that these were the people of God.

First of all, their big attraction is a universal Armageddon —coming any day now—when all except Jehovah's Witnesses will be destroyed—that is, annihilated. But perhaps the reader might better understand all this if he reads the Watch Tower Society's "statement of faith", formerly found in the front of every issue of *The Watchtower* magazine. Here is how it appeared at that time:

THE BIBLE CLEARLY TEACHES

THAT JEHOVAH is the only true God, from everlasting to everlasting, and is the Maker of heaven and earth and Giver of life to his creatures; that the Word or Logos was the beginning of his creation and his active agent in creating all other things; and that the creature Lucifer rebelled against Jehovah and raised the issue of his universal sovereignty;

THAT GOD created the earth for man, made perfect man for the earth and placed him upon it; that man yielded to unfaithful Lucifer, or Satan, and willfully disobeyed God's law and was sentenced to death; that by reason of Adam's wrong act all men are born sinners and without the right to life;

THAT THE LOGOS was made human as the man Jesus and suffered death in order to produce the ransom or redemptive price for obedient men; that God raised up Christ Jesus divine and exalted him to heaven above every other creature and clothed him with all power and authority as head of God's new capital organization;

THAT GOD'S CAPITAL ORGANIZATION is a Theocracy called Zion, and that Christ Jesus is the Chief Officer thereof and is the rightful King of the new world; that the faithful anointed followers of Christ Jesus are Zion's children, members of Jehovah's organization, and are his witnesses whose duty and privilege it is to testify to Jehovah's supremacy and declare his purpose toward mankind as expressed in the Bible;

2

THAT THE OLD WORLD, or Satan's uninterrupted rule, ended A.D. 1914, and Christ Jesus has been placed by Jehovah upon the throne, has ousted Satan from heaven, and now proceeds to vindicate his name and establish the "new earth";

THAT THE RELIEF and blessings of the peoples can come only by Jehovah's kingdom under Christ, which has begun; that his next great act is to destroy Satan's organization and establish righteousness completely in the earth; and that under the Kingdom the people of good-will surviving Armageddon will carry out the divine mandate to fill the earth" with righteous offspring, and that the human dead in the graves will be raised to opportunities of life on earth.

I did not give the above statement the careful analysis that I should have, and so I was influenced by it considerably. I did not realize what was involved, and even if I had, I would not have been able to counteract it, as I had no real knowledge of the Bible. So I believed everything they said, just as all new converts to the Witnesses do. Here is why: You accept the "faithful and wise servant" of Matthew 24:45, 46 as the "servant" of Isaiah 43:10. You are told this "servant" is the Watch Tower Society. Once you accept this, then you will accept anything they tell you, because of the authority you are led to believe they have over you.

Being convinced therefore that this was God's organization, I studied all publications of theirs upon which I could lay my hands. This prepared me to answer questions people would ask me concerning the Society's origin, etc. I studied many of Charles Taze Russell's books and ready many of the lectures given by the Bible Students (they were not called "Jehovah's Witnesses" until 1931) in Russell's time at their conventions.

On the surface, the organization seemed not to have much to offer. Jehovah's Witnesses were not an educated people by any means. They were intolerant and narrow minded. They seemed to think they had a right to tell others what to do, as well as when and how to do it. But I overlooked all this because I felt that from the standpoint of the Scriptures, it was God's organization, and that settled that. *He* would there-

18

fore be the judge, and not I. I concerned myself mainly with mastering the doctrine, and gaining ability to present it to the public and to the Witnesses from the Kingdom Hall platform.

The Witnesses did not appeal to me. As I began to mingle with the younger set, I could see that this did not go very deep with them. It was superficial—yet the young men would rather go to jail than serve their country in the Armed Forces! You see, it was and still is considered unscriptural to wear the uniform of one of the branches of the Armed Forces of any country. Why so?

NEW WORLD VERSUS OLD WORLD GOVERNMENT!

One of elementary things you learn when becoming a Jehovah's Witness is that all governments are of the Devil, and only the Watch Tower organization is exempt from this charge! You are told that it is unscriptural to enter the Armed Forces. Since you are considered an ordained minister (at baptism), you are expected to ask for a clerical exemption from the services.

At the age of twenty I was living in Austin, Minnesota. I registered there for the draft, and requested ministerial exemption. It turned out that they sent me a 1-A classification, but upon appeal I received the desired 4-D classification. This, of course, encouraged me all the more and helped convince me this organization was the right one for me to be in. I remember attending (at a later date) two trials that were held for young men who did not get the desired treatment from the authorities. One was a draft case and the other man was having trouble as a result of doing street witnessing. Such trials always create widespread interest among Jehovah's Witnesses, and confirm the faith of the Witnesses in their organization. And these had that very effect upon me, too.

The current literature of the time (when I came in the organization) was dead set against all *religion*, as well as all constituted authority. Following are some quotations from literature which was available to Witnesses then in the organization. First from the *Consolation* magazine of May 31, 1939. This was written by "Judge" Rutherford, who was president of the Society from shortly after Russell's death until he himself died in 1942. The article is entitled *Religion Rejects Jehovah*:

19

It is aptly stated by Professor Weigle, of Yale: "Jehovah is not a functioning religious term." The reason that his name is not a "functioning religious term" is, because Jehovah is against religion and has expressed His purpose to destroy all religion, that the people of goodwill may know, believe and obey Jehovah God and live.

The June 28, 1939 issue of *Consolation*, under the same title, made it even more emphatic in these words: "There are those who are properly called Jehovah's Witnesses. They are not religionists; for the reason, they do not practice religion." Then, in explanation of what constitutes a religionist, they state:

A religionist is not a witness for Jehovah, for the reason that religion is against God. The mass of the people who follow religion do so because they have been or are deceived by the Devil, the author of religion. It has been difficult for men to resist the temptation placed before them by the Devil in the form of religion. Unless one follows closely the Word of God he is almost certain to fall into the religious trap of Satan.

This made the Watchtower organization very outstanding, of course. Not only this, but we had been talked out of heaven and into the "new world" which, we were promised, was to be "ushered in" any day now! We felt sorry for the poor religionists, and so glad that we were not part of them! Our feelings were well expressed by the *Consolation* magazine, August 5, 1942, page 18:

There are millions of people on the earth today who have been led to believe that because they are members of an earthly religious organization which clergymen called their "church" they are going to heaven. The clergy are the ones who have misled them. Such have not even started on the way to heaven.

And so, deriding all others except ourselves, we felt secure in our pseudo-theocratic society. I thought it was theocratic, at the time. I did not realize how mistaken this assumption was! The showdown was supposed to be Armageddon, when

20

all earthly governments would be wiped out, with the "theocratic government" then taking over the entire world.

The book *The Kingdom Is At Hand*, which I studied first when coming into the organization, contains many statements against all religion(s). Here are some samples. On page 65 we read:

Another line of Adam's descent ran through Seth, born after the assassination of the man of faith, Abel. Seth had a son, Enos. His day is noteworthy. In what way? In that men, who had multiplied considerably by then, organized religion [notice Genesis 4:26], which religion Satan the Devil introduced in Eden to bring about man's fall.

Then from page 74 we get this treatment of the subject: "Babylon on earth became the nursing place of organized religion, which is demonism or demonolatry. All of Babylon's kings, from Nimrod on, practiced religion or devil-worship." Now on page 348 we find material in the same vein:

Let be shocked whoever will, but it is true: Religion leads the rulers and peoples of this earth unto a clash with the King of kings. Those who blindly follow her will be destroyed with her.... Religion will save none of them from the battle of Armageddon. In fact, the King of kings will strike confusion into the ranks of the religion-led united nations, and the political elements will turn their horns of power against the religious organization.

We conclude with this quotation from page 347:

Organized religion, the Babylonish fornicatrix with this world, chooses the postwar creature of international confederation as her king, her Caesar, and she goads its ruling elements on into direct conflict with Jehovah's King on Mount Zion. She deceives them to become anti-christ by their international postwar creature or *beast*.

I soon found that no individual study or research was allowed, but one's knowledge must be limited by what the Watch Tower organization permits him to have. A person could not think beyond that. He could arrive at no conclu-

21

sions that the Watchtower literature had not *already* arrived at! In this way all private thought was discouraged, and the member soon became an automaton.

THE BRAINWASHING COMPLETE!

Within three years my entire outlook on life and God Himself had been completely changed. I truly became a slave mentally to my spiritual overlords. I travelled to various parts of the country and met Jehovah's Witnesses in the South, the Southwest, the West and Central and Northern states. The further away one got from New York, the less the Witnesses seemed to know! But they were all sold on the organization, ignorant though many of them were. It seemed not to matter how little they knew; as long as they were obedient to the organization they were held in good standing by the local company (now called *congregation*).

I often found the Witnesses to be liars, thieves, cheats, lawbreakers and many of them just plain ungodly people! But I had been sold *organization*; and so I merely shrugged it off (while having a tendency to become like the rest!), saying, "God will be their judge—not I!"

I found the young people to be in a rather bad condition, morally. They seemed to have no scruples at all. Anything went, as long as the Society in New York did not hear about it! God did not seem to matter—it was the New York headquarters that could act! Does this seem to indicate that the headquarters is Christian and trying to maintain Christian standards? No. They are the ones who have spawned this entire thing. Now they are finding it difficult to control. Many times lenient company servants (heads of local congregations, now called *congregation servants*) permitted drunkenness and loose living among the congregation's leaders and their wives. All this I overlooked, as did most of the other Witnesses. We were content to let God judge His organization.

So you see the whole thing is NOT based upon sound Scriptural living and teaching, but upon accepting the ORGANIZATION. You accept the organization as your saviour—for, you are taught, the ORGANIZATION will be spared through Armageddon, and you MUST be a part of it in order to escape destruction. Thus you become a part of the *organization-saviour*.

That is what we were to be conscious of constantly. Especially so after the international convention held at Yankee Stadium (which ground they rent from the Knights of Columbus!) in 1950. That was a turning point in the organization. We were told that *The New World Society* was now in full operation. The Society that year began to concentrate on every territory not worked regularly each year. In 1953 (again at Yankee Stadium) a Watchtower catechism-answer-book was released—called *Make Sure Of All Things*. Most Witnesses are stuck when called upon to discuss the Bible if they do not have this book handy.

Since it is their *organization* more than anything else that holds the Witnesses in mental bondage, I would like to go into some details of the organization and its structure. I, like all others, was influenced by the organization everywhere I went. I had to read the Bible through Watchtower glasses in order to get the right slant on its teachings. The next chapter will reveal some of the mechanics of this *New World Society*.

2

Impressions Of The Organization

IT SEEMED LOGICAL

There is a certain feeling one gets from being thought of as different. That feeling Jehovah's Witnesses have. They believe that God is restoring true worship to the earth and that theirs is this worship. This, of course, impressed me. You see, to someone not versed in the Scriptures, all their doctrines sound logical and solid. They believe that they have the final answer to problems that have been with us for centuries. They pontificate on matters such as denying Christ's deity, His second coming, eternal punishment, the trinity, soul, etc. They take Scriptures as they please and throw them together; many times these are unrelated texts, taken out of context—and, sometimes they do not even complete the entire verse!

They use a pet text found at Isaiah 1:18: "Come now, let us reason together, saith the Lord." And so they apply human reason to all their conclusions. They base it upon how *they* would do it if they were God. Naturally, they have to allow for changes that occur from time to time in doctrinal matters. It is as if God changes His mind from time to time, and reverses Himself on some matters! (But that does not bother them.) Whenever the Society pulls something "new" on the Witnesses, it is accepted as "meat in due season" coming from the "Lord's table". I know, for I too was a generally docile, brainwashed follower, as gullible as the others.

Another thing which impressed me: Very few people seemed capable of counteracting our "logic"! This made it appear all the more sound. And so, based on the reasoning of our own minds, we pursued our "religion of logic". Did I say *religion*? Yes! The Watch Tower Society later got around to accepting the term *religion,* after making such a fuss over it during and immediately after World War II!

We were told that the titles assumed by clerics and members of church boards was unscriptural, and that was why *we* were called *servants.* Quoting *The Watchtower* magazine of October 15, 1944, page 315, we read:

> To be organized for the final work in these latter days there must likewise be a governing body under Christ. But "elective elders" and men with other high sounding ecclesiastical titles as "bishop", etc., are out of the question. Those in the religious organizations who bear such titles act as hindrances and opposers to the final work being done by Jehovah's Theocratic organization.

Being sold on the idea that we were in "God's organization", we could thereby assume without much difficulty that members of the clergy were our main opponents. IF their doctrines were of the Devil, then they were in "the Devil's organization". It was as simple as that! In order to get the "truth", they had to get it from Jehovah's Witnesses!

Further brainwashing on the subject of Christendom is found in *The Watchtower* magazine of September 1, 1945, page 260:

> Instead of being one in Christ, and also instead of being one with God through his Christ, "Christendom" is in the same position toward Jehovah God as are the Jews, whom she has persecuted for more than a thousand years. She is in a worse position, because she professes to follow Christ and to be called by his name. She is rejected of Jehovah God, as much so as the Jewish organizations.

With good reason, therefore, Jehovah's Witnesses decline to have any connections with "Christendom" or to be party to her controversies, her political and religious crimes, and her confusing jangle of religions. Taking their stand with Jehovah's greatest witness, Christ Jesus, and with all other faithful witnesses of Jehovah of olden time, they courageously declare His Word against "Christendom". They warn the people that she is cast off from God.

That is the reason they come to your door! They want to warn you to get out of Christendom (even if you aren't in it!) and become one of them; thereby you *might* get through Armageddon! You might wonder how anyone would expect to win people over with an attitude like that. It is much easier than it seems. It is all based on being impressed by the organization. As you can see by now, this word *organization* is a word much overworked by the Witnesses. To them, *everyone* is in some kind of an organization! They think that because persons are attracted to *their* organization by its outward actions and professions, that people are attracted to the churches for the same reasons. You cannot tell a Jehovah's Witness otherwise!

Whatever the organization says goes. Here is more brainwash fodder, found in *The Watchtower* magazine of October 15, 1946, page 316:

Regardless of the optimistic, rosy promises of the leaders of Christendom, there is no morning of future brightness and prosperity for her. Why not? Because these religious, political and commercial and military leaders of hers speak not according to God's Word. They speak contrary to His law and testimony which apply to this day of decision. They speak according to the traditions of the dead fathers of the past, and also speak according to the "doctrines of demons" in these latter times.

WHAT ABOUT JESUS CHRIST?

Most Jehovah's Witnesses think nothing of the Lord Jesus Christ. I was one of them, and I know. To them Christ is only a subordinate to God, and a member of the "theocratic organization"! Actually, they teach the old Arian heresy about Christ. Here is a quotation from *The Watchtower* magazine of May 15, 1946 regarding their thoughts on Him:

The true shepherd, Christ Jesus, had a spirit existence in heaven prior to coming down to lay down his life for the sheep. From the time that Jehovah God created and brought forth this only begotten Son of His the Father has known him, and likewise the Son, the Good Shepherd, has known the Father. They had a mutual confidence in each other.

26

Further, *The Watchtower* magazine of October 1, 1958 infers that Christ was a sinner by placing him in the category of sinners. That issue, page 605 states under the sub-title *JESUS, THE FIRST TO BE BORN AGAIN:*

To completely vindicate his Father's name, establish God's kingdom and destroy Satan, Jesus would have to be a glorious powerful spirit creature. To this end JESUS HAD TO BE BORN AGAIN from the spirit. (Emphasis mine).

By thus lowering the Son of God, they have just God (the Father only, they believe) and the organization that matters. In this manner they have exalted the organization in the eyes of the Jehovah's Witness members.

Jehovah's Witnesses will say to inquirers that *they* use the Watch Tower Society as *their* instrument to carry out God's will. The reverse of the matter is true. The Society uses the Witnesses to carry out *it's* world-wide literature campaigns. This does not occur to them, however. *The Watchtower* magazine, September 1, 1961, page 539, brings this to the fore in the article "Staying Awake as Approved Slaves".

ORGANIZATION STRUCTURE

Here is the set-up of the Watch Tower system as it exists today. At the bottom is what is known as the "kingdom publisher". He is the person you face (in most cases) at your door. He devotes week-ends and an occasional evening to this work. He receives the literature at the Kingdom Hall at rates slightly under the price he asks of you. He reports all activity to the local Kingdom Hall for their permanent record.

The pioneer could be considered the next step up. He devotes 100 hours a month to this work. He receives seven magazines a week free, pays three cents each for all others. He gets the fifty-cent bound books for ten cents each. He obtains all other books sold by the Society at considerably reduced rates. He reports all activity directly to the Watch Tower Society. I was a pioneer on three occasions.

Up the ladder we next meet the special pioneer. He devotes 150 hours a month to the work. Literature rates same as regular pioneer. In contrast to the regular pioneer who must work

27

part-time to make a living, the special pioneer is sustained by the Society.

Circuit servants (who are in the special pioneer category) maintain charge over approximately twenty congregations, which they visit every six months for one or two weeks. His superior is the district servant, whose superior is the branch servant. Over him is the zone servant and on top, the Watch Tower Society composed of seven directors, of which the president has the final word.

Each Kingdom Hall has seven overseers. Each is in charge of a certain field or function. Territory, book room, magazine department, Bible study, ministry school, congregation servant, and his assistant are the seven offices. Then there is the area study conductor—the one who maintains charge over the local neighbourhood group of Witnesses. A Kingdom Hall may have any number of these, usually two to twenty.

With all these eyes on you it is difficult to maintain any individuality whatsoever, so you just give up. When I was a school servant ("ministry school" conductor) I would help write lectures for various speakers. I would be sure that what went into their speeches coincided with current Watchtower viewpoints. They were not allowed to interject anything that did not square with what the Watch Tower Society taught *at the moment*. (You never knew when they were going to change, however!)

"WATCHTOWER TRUTH"

Anything coming from the Watch Tower Society is taken as truth, regardless of what it is! *Everything* that comes from any other source is falsehood, regardless of what it is! So there is little hope of impressing a Jehovah's Witness with anything. My viewpoint as a J. W. was that *all* truth from God came via this organization, and all else was darkness. So, no matter *what* a person told me, it did not impress me, because *I* had the *truth* and *they* did *not*!

Anyone with an open mind will admit that truth is universal, and for any one group or demoniation to say "we have it all" is utter nonsense. And, as shall be proved later in this book, the Watch Tower Society has but very little truth. However, I did not know that *then*. I remember twice making the statement: "If this is not the truth then there is no God!" *That's* how sure I was that it was the truth.

"Watch Tower truth" changes from time to time. Quoting *The Watchtower* magazine of October 15, 1954, we read on page 638:

> No other organization has shown this flexibility to alter its views, to keep up with changing times, to be alert to the increased light that comes from Jehovah from the temple, for other groups are bound by their centuries-old creeds.

This changing of doctrine is done lest the Witnesses get tired of hearing the same old thing over and over again. Also, it makes it appear as if they are getting rid of false doctrines! If they were to do *this*, they would have to abandon practically all that they believe! They would have to start over again, for there would not be much left!

HOW FALSE IMPRESSIONS ARE CREATED

Many of the impressions of the Society that the Witnesses create are definitely false. I know this from practical experience. I engaged in such activity for ten years. Much of it is merely assumed by the J. W., with no real evidence to offer. For example, in the book *Qualified To Be Ministers,* used by Jehovah's Witnesses in their service meetings, we read under the chapter "Answering Questions":

> "We have our own literature" is a remark often met. Of such persons, ask questions as to what their literature has to say on such things as the time of the end, the new world, opportunity for life in a new earth, etc. Then demonstrate how the Watchtower publications are a product of much research, not merely church news or a reiteration of certain creeds, but a progressive, advancing study of the Bible as its sacred secrets are being rapidly revealed during the unparalleled events of our day.

A false impression is created because: All of the above points are *assumed* to be correct by the J. W. They think there is one final answer to it all, and this is it! They lead the listener to believe that the Watchtower publications have profound truths to disclose. Many times persons will get into the organization and not realize until years later just how they were fooled. Blindly accepting everything and anything the organization hands them is their downfall.

Here is how the deception is to be used when making a revisit on a book placement—called a *back-call* by the Witnesses. Quoting the above book, chapter titled "Return Visits", on page 208:

> To prepare for return visits, the first call may sometimes be concluded with a remark of this nature: "You are now entitled to a free demonstration of how to use this book." Or, "You are entitled to one hour's free instruction during this month," or, "I will be in this area again next week and would like to talk with you some more then."

This is not integrity. It is cheap deception. You would think that persons who are supposed to be Christian educators would avoid using these tactics. This same deception is used to get prospective converts started in the book selling work. The above book, under "Directing Interest To The Organization", reads on page 217 and 218:

> The best way to get your student in the service is to invite him in the door-to-door work. Continually relate the joyful experiences you are having. Radiate the happiness it gives. Describe the reactions of the people to the message.
>
> If they accompany you in the service, do your very best in witnessing. Display the proper attitude. If rebuffs or opposition is encountered at the doors, explain that this is evidence of the great dividing work Jehovah is now carrying on, with his King Christ Jesus separating the sheep and the goats.

You see how clever the brainwashing is? They must do unto others as they themselves have been done unto. The above-recommended attitudes to be displayed are for putting on a good show for the benefit of the newcomer, who is supposed to think everything is peaches and cream!

THEY IMPRESS THEMSELVES

Jehovah's Witnesses are constantly praising themselves and

relating how wonderful they are. They impress one another. Of course, this is *not* done as a result of individual free thought; oh no! The organization has taught them to thus impress themselves! The above-quoted book says on page 360:

> Jehovah's Witnesses do not hate persons in the world, but show love by trying to help them. In fact, they are anxious to co-operate with anyone who is desirous of knowing more concerning the Bible. . . .

However, anyone who is *really* desirous of learning the Bible can easily show *that* statement to be a lie!

HOW IMPRESSIVE THEIR ORIGINATOR?

The Watchtower magazine of July 15, 1950, page 212, states the following concerning the founder of the Watch Tower Society, Charles Taze Russell:

> In his teens Charles Taze Russell, the editor, had been a member of the Congregational Church and a strong believer in the doctrine of eternal torture of damned human souls in a hell of literal fire and brimstone. . . . But when trying to reclaim an acquaintance, an infidel, to Christianity, he himself was routed from his sectarian position and driven into scepticism.
>
> Hungrily he began investigating the heathen religions in search of the truth on God's purpose and man's destiny. Proving all these unsatisfactory and before giving up religious investigation altogether, he took up the search of the Holy Scriptures FROM A SCEPTIC'S VIEWPOINT, now untrammeled by the false religious doctrines of the sectarian systems of Christendom. (Emphasis mine).

Read carefully the above quotation. Do you see what it says? Being free from the "false doctrines of the sectarian systems of Christendom" left him a *sceptic*—NOT a Christian! And as such—a NON-CHRISTIAN SCEPTIC—he began the group that blossomed into the Watch Tower Society of Jehovah's Witnesses!

It is no wonder that present-day Jehovah's Witnesses say

nothing about their founder! The less they know about him the better—for the Society! Russell perjured himself in court in front of his brethren and revealed himself as a fraud (claiming he knew Greek when he could not even read the alphabet!) Having previously *denied* the charge that he had no knowledge of Latin, Hebrew, philosophy, and systematic theology, he later *admitted under oath* that he had never studied in these fields, and that his formal education had ended at age fourteen.

The average J. W. whom you meet today is just as dishonest and fraudulent. He claims to be a scholar, which he definitely isn't. Neither is he a student of the Scriptures. At best he is a devout student of the Watch Tower publications.

MY PERSONAL IMPRESSIONS THROUGH THE YEARS

As time went by I could see many of these things, but I had to keep them to myself. Many other brothers shared my opinions (we spoke about them in secret) but we could not voice our opinions to others because of fear. I could see that with most of the Witnesses this was a superficial thing. As for my own life, I knew this religion went only so deep and there it stopped.

I knew I was a sinner—no one had to tell me that. And I knew also that all these works—door to door, platform speeches, book studies, convention work, etc., had not removed a single sin. I knew there was no real power to this; that in the end I was still the same sinner as I had always been, in spite of my being a Jehovah's Witness. But, like all the other Witnesses, I placed all hopes *and* responsibility on the *organization*, and let it go at that. Very seldom were we challenged at the door by persons who asserted that either Christ has removed these sins through His shed blood, or we will die in those sins—works being unable to remove them. In the ten years that I spent in that work, I was challenged only four times. The fourth occasion is related in chapter six.

FINAL IMPRESSIONS

The final impressions of the organization that I took with me are not fondly remembered. They include the most unpleasant experiences of my life. Some will be related in chap-

32

ter eight. It is expected that the average J. W. reading this will dismiss it all as the impressions of one who has turned unfaithful and is now just a castaway. Be that as it may, you cannot escape the convictions of your own heart. If you think you can, just try it sometime! And it must be remembered that I did not ask for these things to happen. They just happened.

Jehovah's Witnesses are expert backbiters and liars. They have no scruples when it comes to that. And if one from their midst decides from his own conscience to leave their organization and go over to another faith, they angrily turn against and upon him. All sorts of stories are spread. Thus they express their true nature!

I found that the majority of Witnesses either stay for approximately five or ten years and then leave, or else remain and become "old timers". If they grow disappointed and leave they are bitter against all religion and usually remain that way. It is a pitiful state for a person to be in. His ears are stopped entirely to the gospel and he remains, in his deafness, unheedful to the call of Jesus Christ.

All of the so-called "brotherhood" is so much pretence. The Watch Tower leaders (who are all white men) claim that all races are accepted equally within their organization. Thousands of non-Caucasians flock into the organization for this one fact alone. They should hear their white brothers talking when they are not around! They should hear what the white Witnesses say to one another about Negroes and others in the organization! I feel so sorry for those who have fallen for this "equality" line, for it is all a put-on show!

I call upon you Witnesses who are non-white: DO NOT BE SO THOROUGHLY DECEIVED! You should look behind the scenes and see some of the things *I* have seen. Look into the Bible also and see—this is not Christianity! I urge you all to pray earnestly that as you read this book your eyes shall be opened and you shall see the glory of the truth shining forth from the throne of your precious Saviour.

3

3

A Life Of Constant Debating

CLERGY RESPONSIBLE FOR DEBATE!

Arguing with everybody regardless of what they believe has its drawbacks. Sometimes it's a strain on the imagination to believe every other person on earth is wrong except you (and other Jehovah's Witnesses!) Yet, if you are to remain a J. W. you must consider everyone else as deceived. Of course, we placed the *blame* for their being wrong on the *clergy*. Quoting *The Watchtower* magazine of May 15, 1950, we read on page 151.

> Jehovah's witnesses not only bear the clear, truthful doctrines of the Bible about God's kingdom, but they have lived up to the name BY OPPOSING THE FALSE DOCTRINES OF THE CLERGY.... Unlike the clergy, they have never been false impersonators. (Emphasis mine.)

The truth of the matter is that Jehovah's Witnesses are the deceivers? Why? Because they themselves have been deceived by their organizational headquarters. If you should doubt this ask any J. W. this question: If it were not for the organization, would there by any Jehovah's Witnesses?

DEBATING AS SLAVES

We *had* to constantly debate because we were mere slaves, as has already been mentioned. We were told so by the Society! Here is how they put it, from *The Watchtower* magazine, April 15, 1950, page 119:

The important yet humble position occupied by a servant or SLAVE in the Lord's organization was looked down upon with scorn and contempt by these puffed-up and pompous ones who presumptuously assumed shepherdhood over the sheep. Proud and haughty, they pushed aside the privilege of being servants, installed themselves as clergy (a class not provided or arranged for either by Christ or the apostles), and took upon themselves flattering titles.... (Emphasis mine.)

These words of the Lord Jesus apparently escape their attention: "NO LONGER DO I CALL YOU SERVANTS; FOR THE SERVANT KNOWETH NOT WHAT HIS LORD DOETH: BUT I HAVE CALLED YOU FRIENDS" (John 15:15). Of course, that close relationship between Christ and the Christian does not exist for the J. W., and so he believed it is God's arrangement for him to be somebody else's slave.

The Watchtower publications were our medium of debate. We could not debate our own convictions, but only what we found in the printed material. Quoting *Consolation* magazine of December 29, 1937, page 18:

Your Bible AND THE BOOKS showing you where to find the texts, which books are published by THE WATCHTOWER BIBLE & TRACT SOCIETY, will enable every person who tries to get an understanding of the truth and to be guided in the right way. (First emphasis my own.)

Notice how the above statement makes it appear as if the Watchtower publications are only used to locate Bible texts? This is not so. The Witnesses do not use that many Biblical texts. Much of their conversation has been taken from current Watchtower material. This shows the tremendous influence of Watchtower material on their minds. I know this from my personal experience.

"HOW TO ARGUE"

Naturally, to be able to go through many years of arguing and debating successfully takes advance preparation. That is where the Jehovah's Witnesses have it over the average church member. The J. W. is prepared by means of training and the church member is not. A Christian should prepare himself to give a logical and clear testimony of what Christ has done for him, or expect his words to land on deaf ears. Following is an example of material used by Jehovah's Witnesses in preparing themselves for the task of debating. From *Qualified To Be Ministers,* under the chapter "Argumentation", found on page 198:

> Every proposition to be argued has special issues that support it. If the affirmative side cannot prove all these issues, then the argument to support the proposition fails. Analyze, get at the root of the matter. Often a proposition hangs on one or two major issues. Select the issues you know are important and do not waste time by being led off into every issue the opponent brings up. As an illustration, someone may say, "Jehovah's Witnesses should salute the flag". The issues would be: Is it required by God? or, Does it violate the law? and, Is it proper and necessary from the viewpoint of patriotism?

The entire "ministry" of Jehovah's Witnesses is based upon such argumentation.

ARGUING AGAINST THE TRINITY

This is one of the favourite subjects of Jehovah's Witnesses, and the one on which they are least prepared to argue! This subject involves the deity of Christ and the personality of the Holy Spirit. At the moment we shall only consider the method used by the Witnesses in debating these matters. When I first came into association with the J. W.'s I was faced with arguments such as this one, taken from *The Kingdom Is At Hand,* page 50:

> Only the religious trinitarians are presumptuous enough to claim, without Scripture basis, that two other persons are equal with Jehovah God; but Jesus does not himself claim to be one of such persons. For his humble course Jesus has been exalted higher than he was before becoming a man, even next to God himself.

Yet on page 46 of this same book they admit that the name JESUS (*Jeshua* in Hebrew) means JEHOVAH THE SAVIOUR! Now note the following paragraph taken from page 46; it gives a lot of material without a single Scripture even being mentioned!

At the time of his beginning of life he was created by the everlasting God, Jehovah, without the aid or instrumentality of any mother. In other words, he was the first and direct creation of Jehovah God. As such he was Jehovah's *only begotten* Son. He was the start of God's creative work, and all that would next be brought into existence would be after-creations. Jehovah God could use this only begotten Son to create such other things, because this Son was the direct offspring of the Almighty One and hence was a mighty one, or a god.

ARGUING AGAINST HELL

The book *Let God Be True*, published in 1946 and later revised, has been the mainstay of the Witnesses on doctrine. Quoting from page 99 of the 1952 revised edition from the chapter "Hell, a Place of Rest in Hope":

The doctrine of a burning hell where the wicked are tortured eternally after death cannot be true, mainly for four reasons: (1) It is wholly unscriptural; (2) it is unreasonable; (3) it is contrary to God's love, and (4) it is repugnant to justice. From this it is appreciated more that Gehenna is the condition of destruction where the Devil, his demons, and all human opposers of Jehovah's theocratic government will go and from which condition there is no resurrection or recovery.

ARGUING AGAINST THE SOUL

Jehovah's Witnesses believe that the soul is a living physical body, whether animal or human. Typical of arguments the Watch Tower Society uses to "prove" this is the following from *Let God Be True*, in the chapter "What is Man", on page 70:

The fact that the human soul is mortal can be amply proved by a careful study of the Holy Scriptures. An immortal soul cannot die, but God's Word, at Ezekiel 18:4, says concerning humans: "Behold, all souls are mine; as the soul of the father, so also the soul of the son is mine: the soul that sinneth, it shall die."

Did they say "a careful study of the Holy Scriptures"? Let us be just a little more careful than *they* have been and read further on in the eighteenth chapter of Ezekiel:

But if a man be just, and do that which is lawful and right ... he shall surely live, saith the Lord God. (18:5, 9).
But if the wicked will turn from all his sins that he hath committed ... he shall surely live, he shall not die. In his righteousness that he hath done he shall live. (18:21, 22).
Again, when the wicked man turneth away from his wickedness that he hath committed, and doeth that which is lawful and right, HE SHALL SAVE HIS SOUL ALIVE. (18:27).

ARGUING AGAINST THE RANSOM

To Jehovah's Witnesses Jesus Christ is only a man who gave them a chance to work out their own salvation. They believe that he atoned only for Adam's disobedience, humanity's "original sin"—though not for the man Adam himself. (Adam was given no opportunity of salvation because his sin was done knowingly and deliberately.) They do not believe that Christ atoned for our personal sins, but only for our disobedience in Adam. Quoting *Let God Be True*, in the chapter "A Ransom in Exchange for Many", on page 116:

That perfect human life which Jesus laid down in death is that valuable thing which accomplishes the purchase of what Adam's sin of disobedience lost for all his offspring.

Along that same line of argument, we quote from page 117, same book:

We see by sin Adam lost perfect human life and was justly sentenced to death and eventually died, and all his

38

descendants inherited sin and death from him. God made his beloved Son a perfect man, and Jesus was faithful, went into death, and was afterward resurrected by God's power and exalted to heaven, there presenting to God the merit or value of his perfect human life.

Coming to a conclusion on this matter, the above book states on page 120:

> The ransom places upon those who want to benefit from it an obligation and a marvellous privilege. "The sting producing death is sin" (1 Corinthians 15:56, *NW*). So in order for men to be saved from death due to being stung by sin they must inform themselves of God's mercy through Christ Jesus and then have faith in the provision He has made. This faith means to rely on such provisions confidently, to give God all credit for it, and then to demonstrate this conviction by devoting oneself to God and by informing others about the ransom.

In this manner they steer persons into the door-to-door work. Notice it is not belief into repentance and salvation; just belief and then works! They believe Christ provided the type of ransom where we are enabled to work out our *own* salvation.

ARGUING AGAINST CHRIST'S RETURN

Jehovah's Witnesses believe that Christ "returned" invisibly in 1914. Quoting again from *Let God Be True* on "Christ's Return", on page 201:

> For many years prior to 1914 earnest Bible students [Russellites] understood that the year 1914 marked the end of the Gentile times or the "appointed times of the nations". That date marked the beginning of the "time of the end" of Satan's rule, and therefore the time when Christ Jesus the righteous Ruler of the new world received control.

Jehovah's Witnesses think they are reacting to this in the manner described below, from the same book, page 206:

Today persons of good will from all nations are taking their stand for Jehovah's Theocracy. This "great crowd" of other sheep are welcoming the new King by engaging in the Kingdom proclamation, even as the multitude welcomed Jesus on his triumphal ride into Jerusalem. (Revelation 7:9-17, *NW*; Luke 19: 37-40). Back there the Pharisees wanted the multitude rebuked. So today religious leaders try to silence and suppress the message. Their efforts have failed and will fail.

ARGUING AGAINST JUDGMENT AFTER DEATH

Jehovah's Witnesses believe that the coming judgment will be the millennium—the "thousand year reign of Christ", as they put it. Quoting a paragraph in the *Let God Be True* book, in the chapter "The Judgment Day", we read on page 284:

Seeing that the millenial judgment day has reference to only one specific judgment of Jehovah, it is important for us to ascertain what judgment this is, to whom it applies. Then, to ascertain who the judge will be, we must consider his qualifications, how he will execute judgment, and what the result will be when completed.

Then on page 292 we read the following regarding the judge of this judgment day:

The Scriptures say he served God his Father with a godly fear and learned obedience by the things which he suffered, and that hence those who meet with his favourable judgment will be granted everlasting life.

Jehovah's Witnesses believe they will be judged favourably because of the works they performed in this present life.

ARGUING AGAINST REGENERATION

The last chapter in the *Let God Be True* book is titled "Life Transformed By Making the Mind Over". Here are portions of this chapter from page 306:

Our Creator, who constructed our intricate brain and gifted us with mind, understands its mechanism and operation better than any college psychologist or psycho-analyst of this so-called "brain age". Instantly he detects any bent of man's mind and knows what it will surely lead to. So he encourages good leanings and warns us of the fatal consequences that follow an evil bent.

He can best help us make our minds over so as to transform our lives in expectation of the approaching new world. How? Why, by giving us his Holy Word in writing; by giving us his spirit or active force to make that Word clear to us; and by providing us his theocratic organization, his "faithful and discreet slave", to help us understand that Word.

Notice the degrading of the Holy Spirit to "active force" and the position the organization takes in His place? Quite contrary to John 14:26, 15:26 and 16:13. Here is more from that chapter, quoting from page 309:

When we transform our minds by making them over according to the knowledge we get from the Bible by which God speaks to us, then we prove to ourselves the "good and acceptable and complete will of God".

Notice that it is a self-transformation, quite the opposite of Romans 12:2 and Ephesians 4:23. Here is their "hope" as expressed on page 310, same book:

Let us keep our minds new by talking to others the things we have learned from God's Word and thereby exalt him and his kingdom and thus help those who listen to us toward salvation.

Then, whether we die before the universal war of Armageddon or whether we survive it under divine protection; whether we come up in the resurrection of the dead or we live through this old world's complete end, we shall enter the new world with a mind made over according to God's will and joyfully in tune with the glorious new world.

The above speaks for itself. You can see clearly the pitiful state these folk are in. They believe by making their minds over they can thus eradicate the evil bent of the mind and remove sin. Their salvation is never sure, of course, so they must keep on that ever-turning treadmill of works-by-book-selling!

Jehovah's Witnesses keep themselves in line by constantly thinking on these matters. They constantly talk themselves into it, deeper and deeper. They convince themselves and each other. They are constantly devising ways of improving the presentation of their message. To them it is strictly all educational and intellectual. Everything to run on a business-like basis.

AGAINST ALL PIETY

Jehovah's Witnesses do not *worship* God. In the ten years that I was one of them, we never held a worship service. There is no reverence for God, no awe of Him in their hearts. I always sensed that something was missing in this respect. We could not worship Jesus Christ. That was strictly forbidden! Having downgraded Him to a creature, He was just an underling of God to all of us.

For a "hymn book" we used "Songs to Jehovah's Praise", a book of ninety-one songs. They extol the works of the organization and the individual tasks performed by Jehovah's Witnesses. No adoring words to God or His Son. Just adoring words for the organization!

Jehovah's Witnesses will never kneel to pray. They have no prayer meetings or devotional programmes. Prayer is offered in a perfunctory way, before and after meetings. They all say the same thing. A standard is set, and everyone follows it automatically.

NO PUBLIC DEBATES

Jehovah's Witnesses, surprisingly, will not hold a public debate! Private debates, yes; but they seem to shy away from anything of a public nature in this category. As famous as they are for debating, you would think this would be a favourite! The reason they do not debate publicly is that they do not feel that sure of themselves. The Watch Tower Society discourages it because they realize that no J. W. can stand up against anyone who knows the Bible well.

Continual propagandizing is necessary to hold Jehovah's Witnesses in line. As long as the Society can keep them talking it feels they will stay put. As long as they are convinced that there is only one answer to all questions, and that *they* have this answer, Witnesses are in little danger of straying.

There is a basic pattern followed by the Society to thus keep the Witnesses in line and in organizational thinking. It is very subtle and realized by few. Naturally, the one deceived hardly ever recognizes the fact that he *is* deceived. When he does, it comes as a blow. The following chapter will include a more complete discussion of this subject.

4

How The New World Society Operates

OPPOSED TO CONVENTIONAL CHRISTIANITY

The New World Society's outlook is idealism personified. It comes to be such because of the manner in which they use the Scriptures. They will rationalize, spiritualize, or humanize as it best suits them. Also, they are very much opposed to the conventional, historic Christian faith with its stress upon the individual and his relation to God. In place of it they have substituted organization. Without this organization they could not exist. Reading *The Watchtower* magazine of December 1, 1947, we find this on page 356:

> The identifying of ourselves with the Theocratic organization results in priceless benefits to us. The working together at doing the divine will benefits all of us co-operating together. We receive the help of one another in doing God's work. We get the stimulation that comes from associating with one another. THUS THE ORGANIZATION MEANS STRENGTH TO US. It means the UNIFYING of us for the sake of working with greater effectiveness. It also means PROTECTION to us in this wicked world. (Emphasis mine.)

It is in this manner that they escape from reality. They have banded themselves within this organization for protection (not salvation!) It has become their strength in lieu of the Holy Spirit.

They are opposed to the structure of the church. *The Watchtower* magazine, June 15, 1958, page 359, states:

The fact of the matter is that the very profession or vocation of a Christian clergy is without Scriptural foundation or precedent. The clergy-laity distinction was wholly unknown by Christians of the first century.

They operate on the principle that the historic church errs in permitting paid expounders of the gospel. But in doing so they forget 1 Corinthians 9:4, 7, 13, 14.

PONTIFICAL INSPIRATION

While the Watchtower Society will not lay claim to special inspiration in their interpretation of the Scriptures, nevertheless something out of the ordinary *is* claimed by them. It is rather difficult to explain, since they themselves have never explained it! Actually, it creates quite a paradox. In what way?

Well, when the Witness receives his book or latest magazine from the Society he is expected to accept whatever is contained therein as truth, even previous to his reading it! The material is held to contain no errors of doctrine whatsoever *at the moment of writing*. The Society cannot then err! The individual Witness, however, does not possess this infallible insight which the Watchtower Society has for writing such material.

Now if the J. W. really and truly accepts the material in that vein, he is recognizing the Society as being composed of some sort of spiritual supermen. Yet he is told that they differ in no manner whatsoever from himself. Yet they receive the privilege of being able to produce the correct interpretation of Scriptures at will, which privilege the individual J. W. is deprived of. How do they possess what they are not supposed to possess that makes them better than the average Witness?

On the other hand, if the J. W. receiving this literature does *not* receive it as truth until his investigation satisfies him that it *is* truth, he is still holding to the Society's recommendations. He is supposed to "prove all things" and not just receive them blindly. YET HE DARE NOT FIND ONE ERROR IN ANY CURRENT WATCHTOWER MATERIAL! Nor dare he successfully contradict anything the Watch Tower Society ever says!

You see, *at the moment of writing* the material is supposed to be free from error *for the present moment*! Why is this? Because it allows for a future reversal of matters! They call this "present truth" because it is truth today but maybe untruth tomorrow! You never know when it is going to be changed. BUT—only the Watch Tower Society may change it, and only when *they* decide it needs changing. So the present Witnesses are preaching what twenty years from now will be considered in certain respects, as non-truth!

This position is an unusual one and defies description. The writers of the Society are inspired, yet *not* inspired! They proclaim a "truth" that is truth only presently, for today—*not* tomorrow. Why didn't they seek that out in the first place? Why deceive the people and make amends later? Actually it is just a trick to sell the Witnesses the line that they are constantly improving themselves. They just change things around. If they were *really* concerned about teaching people the *truth* they would be forced to completely change nearly all of their doctrines. They would have to admit for those they did not change that it is a toss-up as to which interpretation is the correct one. They are not honest enough to do this, however. They are the sole producers of "truth today that becomes tomorrow's lie".

Everything that is done by Jehovah's Witnesses in the organization must be done the way the Society wants it done. They are the master dictators. Anyone who questions their moves or motives is considered "untheocratic". That means he is not a good organization man. He is thinking for himself, and that is outlawed. He is supposed to overrule his own thoughts and convictions and to give way to the Society's.

And so the problem goes unsolved—but unquestioned. Most of the Witnesses do not think that deeply. They just accept it as it is, and take the rest for granted. This simply shows how easy it is to fool people and lead them like animals to the slaughter.

NO J. W.'S IN THE ARMY

Most people are aware of the stand taken by Jehovah's Witnesses against going into the Armed Forces of any nation. I was one of those who received a ministerial classification, so I was never bothered while I was a Witness. And, by the way, I was not a pioneer when I received it, either! Many persons wonder why the Witnesses take the stand they do. Some attribute it to cowardice or lack of patriotism. Remember this one thing, however: You cannot accuse them of acting according to *individual conscience,* for they do not perform acts as *individuals.* They must do all things *organizationally.*

Here is what I mean: Regardless of what they once previously thought or did not think about their country and flag, they *now* must conform to the standards set for them by the Watchtower Society. Therefore whatever they say or do is determined by what the organization dictates for them to say or do. They have lost all individuality altogether, and are mere automatons of the Society.

The Society teaches that all earthly governments are of the Devil. This causes the Witnesses to lose all respect for civil authority. All branches of the government are viewed alike by them. So one must realize that he is not dealing with people who believe and act as they do because of a decision of their own individually guided consciences, but who have been made what they are by *The New World Society.* They do not make their own decisions, nor do they conclude their own conclusions. This is all done for them by their superiors.

So before you can convince a J. W. that he is wrong, you must first convince him that the Watchtower Society is wrong. Otherwise he considers *himself* to be right because he is obeying the Society who is always right! No matter what he does, you cannot place the responsibility squarely on his shoulders alone, but must recognize the pressure the Society exerts in every decision he makes. Although he may suffer the penalty, he is only doing what he has been told to do.

What if he does not do it? He won't be a Jehovah's Witness very long! This is serious to him, because he believes he is in "God's organization". He makes every effort to remain in good standing within the organization because he has been led to believe that all those outside it are doomed to annihilation at Armageddon.

His stand against entering the Armed Forces is not based on cowardice but on obedience—to his organizational masters. When they pipe he dances. When they call he comes. He is at their order and command.

Quoting from *Let God Be True* book under the chapter "Caeser's Things to Caeser", page 237:

The preaching activity of Jehovah's witnesses entitles them to claim exemption from performing military training and service in the armed forces of the nations in which they dwell. The exempt status of Jehovah's witnesses also relieves them of performing governmental work required of men who conscientiously object to both combatant and non-combatant military service, because Jehovah's witnesses are ministers of the gospel and are not political, academic or religious pacifists.

Comparing their work with that of the clergy, this book states on page 239:

Both the orthodox clergy and some of Jehovah's witnesses were classified as ministers of religion and exempted from military service. So they did not help to win World War II by carrying arms. However, people of all nations were served and greatly comforted by the preaching Jehovah's witnesses did during the war. No truthful person can prove they did not do as much for the people's benefit as the orthodox clergy did.

Notice how they were classified as "ministers of religion"? Compare this with the statements made in their publications against religion. Now they seem *glad* to be a part of "organized religion"!

Their stand against saluting the flag is contained in that same chapter quoted above, page 242:

Regardless of whether all people look on the flag-salute ceremony as religious or sacred, it is just the same a political ceremony whereby the symbol, the flag, is saluted or bowed down to religiously. This is an act that ascribes salvation to the national emblem and to the nation for which it stands. Through the salute the saluter impliedly declares that his salvation comes from the thing for which the flag stands, namely, the nation symbolized by the flag.

Jehovah's Witnesses believe that there is no salvation outside their organization. No one can be a Jehovah's Witness independent of their organization. They believe in the supreme authority of the Watch Tower Society in all matters pertaining to the organization and religious doctrine. They believe that an excommunicant is cast off from God eternally. The decisions of the Watch Tower Society are accepted by Jehovah's Witnesses as God's decisions. What they bind on earth is bound in heaven.

So, according to Jehovah's Witnesses, salvation comes only via their organization. They have always been severely critical of the Roman Catholic Church, yet they have copied its organizational pattern! The average J. W. has blinded himself to this fact. This is first-class hypocrisy—practicing what you criticize others for doing.

They do not believe that salvation can be obtained by means of the death, burial and resurrection of Jesus Christ, which we call regeneration (Titus 3:5). Instead, you obtain your own salvation by becoming an active member of their organization. They do not believe that salvation can be obtained in this present life. Rather, you are supposed to spend this entire life *gaining* salvation, which you will receive in the *next* life (on earth, in the "new world"). As to why Jesus died, the book *From Paradise Lost to Paradise Regained* explains their beliefs on that. Quoting from the chapter "Why God's Son Died and Was Raised to Life Again", page 142:

> Why did God let his loving Son die? For more than one good reason. One reason was because of the question, "Who is the supreme ruler of all creation?" Satan had said that human creatures would not stay true to God as the Ruler of all creation. Another good reason why God let his Son suffer and die was that in this way "he learned obedience" (Hebrews 5:8). True, Jesus always had been obedient, but would he be obedient under a great test? By being obedient even when it meant suffering and death, Jesus showed that he could be depended on ever after. He showed himself worthy of the highest place God could give any of his creatures.

You see, to Jehovah's Witnesses, Jesus is only a creature,

as we all are. Note the further reasons given for his death as found on page 143 of this book:

But could not a loving God simply have forgiven the debt of sin and set men free? No, he could not. Why not? Because God had said that the wage sin pays is death. . . .

However, God could arrange for the price to be paid by another who was willing and able to do so. In this way those who suffered wrongly because of Adam's sin could have an opportunity for life.

Because Jesus had God as his Father, he was a perfect man. As a perfect man he had the right to life. By willingly laying down his human life he could use its right to buy back the worthy ones of Adam's children.

Please note: He gave only an *opportunity* for "worthy ones"—not salvation for unworthy sinners (which we all are). They believe that *knowledge* and *works*, not *salvation*, leads to life. Quoting the above book on page 243: "Why is this knowledge so valuable? It is so valuable because it shows the way to endless life in happiness." This is a modern gnostic heresy. And it parallels in many ways the Arian heresy which the Church rejected early in its history.

IS JESUS A CREATED ANGEL?

Jehovah's Witnesses think so. Quoting from *Your Will Be Done On Earth*, page 311: "Yet a Son of God is mentioned in Daniel 12:1. Who? Michael." Pages 312 and 313: "Michael begins to rein as king in heaven during the final years of the king of the north, or 'at the time'. That time God has marked as A.D. 1914. . . . Since Jesus Christ glorified is Michael the great prince of Daniel's people. . . ." Page 315: "Is this Michael the resurrected, glorified and enthroned Jesus Christ? Yes."

The reader might compare the above with Hebrews 1:5-10; 5:5-10; 7:1-21. This puts a complete reversal to the above matters. More will be said on this subject in chapter twelve.

REASON VERSUS BELIEF

Regarding the Holy Spirit, *Awake!* magazine of February 8,

1954, under "Christendom's Pagan Beliefs" (page 25), states:

> As for the holy spirit, mistranslated "Ghost"; there is no Scriptural basis for considering it a person. It is God's active force by which he accomplishes his purposes, such as inspiring men to write his Word (2 Peter 1:21). While the Bible does at times seem to personify the holy spirit, it is more reasonable to hold that an *impersonal* force used by God would be personified than that thousands of persons could be immersed with an individual, or the individual be poured out upon them as the spirit was at Pentecost.—Acts 2:2, 15-18.

In the above they err on two counts: First, by putting *reason* above the Word of God. Secondly, by assuming that the Holy Spirit, *if* a person, would be a person like unto ourselves. God is both omniscient and omnipresent, and since the Holy Spirit is God (Acts 5:3, 4), *He* is likewise omniscient and omnipresent. If the Bible tells us He was poured out, then He *was* poured out—if on a hundred million people at one time! God should know. If He said so, it *was* so! This requires *faith* to accept—faith *above* reason. It also requires *belief* in God's Word that it teaches the truth, in *spite* of what the Watch Tower Society says to the contrary.

AMBITION DESTROYED

This type of theology and associated brainwashing has caused Jehovah's Witnesses to become deadened to the world they live in, and all individual ambition has been destroyed. They do not care what happens, where it happens, or to whom it happens. They live in a dream world, in a non-existent "theocracy". They have imagined all they believe like a child with its fairy tales.

Once a person's ambition has been destroyed he becomes a most useless person. Such is the average Jehovah's Witness. He is not allowed to do anything useful for anyone except Jehovah's Witnesses. He may not aid in Civil Defence, or sign a petition for a referendum against liquor or gambling, for example. Neither may he contribute money to any cause outside of the Watch Tower circle.

They are not concerned about anyone else's welfare

but their own. A man or woman will walk off from his or her marriage mate, if the other does not become a Jehovah's Witness. Many have left homes and families because of this religion of theirs. Their religion does not give the peace of mind with which a person can live with others of a different faith. There is always friction. There can be no peaceful co-existence between a Jehovah's Witness and one of another faith—the Jehovah's Witness will not have it so!

A person's sense of responsibility is thus removed. I remember a congregation servant who was sent to the Nicetown unit in Philadelphia to replace someone of whom the Society no longer approved. This man served just a short while, then disfellowshipped (excommunicated) everybody in the congregation except his wife and himself! The Society then looked into the matter, reinstated the congregation and disfellowshipped the servant instead! He then disappeared and was never heard of again.

Such is the irresponsible type of life lived by Jehovah's Witnesses. It is not a life to be envied! They are more to be pitied than censured. Only when they come free from the grip the Society holds on them are they free to use their own minds and think the kind of thoughts that deserve thinking.

NO CHRISTMAS OR EASTER

Jehovah's Witnesses will not recognize or celebrate either holiday. *The Watchtower* magazine of December 15, 1954, concludes an article on Christmas with these words: "So it is a choice of accepting Christmas with its spirit and losing God, or accepting God and receiving his spirit and favour and losing Christmas." They are just as much against Easter. The reason is simple: Christ means nothing to them, and therefore they see no reason for recognizing either His birth or His death.

Bible-believing Christians often deplore the many worldly and commercial practices that have become associated with Christmas and Easter through the years. But should they, therefore, decline to set aside times to especially remember Christ's birth, death and resurrection? This would be like a child refusing to honour a loving parent because the parent is dressed in unbecoming clothes.

Jesus Christ becomes precious to a person who has been

saved by this very Christ. Jehovah's Witnesses would not know the difference if Christ had never come. They could get along just as well without Him. They are still slaves to a system of works which is supposed to gain salvation for them.

NO HEAVEN FOR MOST BELIEVERS

They believe that only 144,000 "spiritual Israelites" will ever go to heaven. They get this number from the account given of the Jews united with Messiah on Mount Zion (Revelation, chapters seven and fourteen). They think this is the "heavenly class" and that all others are of an "earthly class". They quote John 10:16: "And other sheep I have, which are not of this fold: them also I must bring, and they shall hear my voice; and there shall be one flock, one shepherd." They think that Christ was differentiating between a "heavenly class" and an "earthly class". Actually He was here showing the calling of both Jews and Gentiles into one flock. This escapes their notice, however.

Quoting the *Let God Be True* book in the chapter "The Congregation of God", page 130:

> Because his true congregation was pictured by the twelve tribes of Israel under Moses, the heavenly congregation is likened to twelve tribes of 12,000 members each, under the greater Moses, Christ Jesus. The congregation, then, is restricted to this select, predestinated number; and in heaven it is made the capital part or ruling body of Jehovah's universal organization.

Of course, none of those claiming to be of the 144,000 can tell you which tribe they are from! Strange indeed; yet they ignorantly believe it because the Watch Tower Society teaches it.

NO HELL FOR THE WICKED

Just as there is no heaven for the non-144,000 righteous, so there is no hell for the irreformable, or wicked. Quoting *Let God Be True* again, on page 98:

> Who is responsible for this God-defaming doctrine of a

hell of torment? The promulgator of it is Satan himself. His purpose in introducing it has been to frighten the people away from studying the Bible and to make them hate God.

How do they get around such episodes as that recorded in Luke sixteen, concerning the rich man and Lazarus? The *Let God Be True* book reads on page 98:

By this PARABLE Jesus uttered a prophecy which has been undergoing its modern fulfillment since A.D. 1919. It has its application to two classes existing on earth today. The rich man represents the ultraselfish class of the clergy of Christendom, who are now afar off from God and dead to his favour and service and tormented by the Kingdom truth proclaimed. Lazarus depicts the faithful remnant of the "body of Christ". These, on being delivered from modern Babylon since 1919, receive God's favour, pictured by the "bosom position of Abraham", and are comforted through his Word. (Emphasis mine.)

And so the Witnesses are totally ruined as to a true understanding of the Bible. Notice how they escape the impact of Jesus' words by labelling the episode a *parable*?

THE CONCLUSION OF IT ALL

These points have been presented herein to show why the Society operates as it does, and why Jehovah's Witnesses do the things they do. It is hoped this will cause sympathy rather than resentment towards the Witnesses. They need the help of Christian people everywhere.

You may wonder why people seem to voluntarily get involved in such a system of thought control. There are many reasons, the first of which is that the J.W.'s find many people who have a gripe against their church. There are many such persons. The Witnesses will blow this up all out of proportion, then capitalize upon it by downing the church entirely. The person who agrees with them unsuspectingly accepts whatever literature the Witness offers. Then on each return visit he is turned further against the church and steered into *The New World Society*.

Then again, some persons feel neglected within the church.

They want attention and no one seems to be giving it to them. Then along comes a J. W. who appears to be keenly interested in them and showers them with attention. The unsuspecting listener permits himself to be talked into their line of thought control, all for the attention he is getting as a result.

Others come from churches where the gospel never was preached. These folk are often inwardly desiring and looking for something better. To them it appears that Jehovah's Witnesses have that "something better". Many find out too late that they do not.

Then there is a class of people who are not members of any church but who want to learn the Bible. I was one of them. They desire to become Christians but do not know the way to Christ. When a J. W. comes to their door with a Bible it looks like a Godsend. They listen to him because he is probably the only one who ever expressed an interest in them and their eternal future.

There is one class of people the Witnesses are not prepared to deal with: Everyone who has been born from above. The J. W.'s are NOT trained in their Kingdom Halls to answer the Christ-centred testimony of one who has been born again. They ARE trained to argue along denominational lines, but are NOT trained to argue successfully against the gospel of Christ! This fact will unfold as you read my own personal testimony further on in this book.

As you can readily see, these people have lost their own souls and have been committed to anonymity. As to the effects this has on the minds of these people we leave the succeeding chapter to tell.

5

Effect Of Anonymity On The Mind

To sell the Witnesses *organization*, rather than individuality, *The Watchtower* magazine of June 15, 1960 says (page 376) under the heading *The Light of Life*:

> Today the New World society of Jehovah's witnesses is this light-bearing organization; it is a citylike organization that is prominent around the globe because its members let their light shine before mankind. In a city there are women as well as men, and all contribute various functions. So in this citylike organization of light bearers all contribute to the light so that the organization can blaze as the greatest light today, as "the light of the world".

You will notice the word *organization* occurs four times in the above quotation, and *city* three times. They are supposed to be the collective "light of the world". All individual worth has been taken away to blend into *organizational* worth. You are not the person you are named; you are a Jehovah's Witness! To be yourself is considered "worldliness" and "false religion" to the Witnesses. You must give up being yourself and become, as it were, anonymous.

Their purpose is to get people out of the churches wherein they were individuals and into this organization where they will be individuals no more! To force their idea that the individual-religion is of the Devil, *The Watchtower* magazine of September 1, 1958, page 519, printed the following:

> How glaring is the unscriptural worldliness of Christen-

dom's churches! Powerful Bible truths have been watered down so that sermons become please-the-crowd speeches.

Naturally, the J.W. views all non-Watch Tower sermons as crowd-pleasing material!

THE MOTHER, FATHER AND DAUGHTER

The above is done to get people out of and actively set against the church. Then, into the organization where they will no longer be individuals. They believe that this loss of individuality and acquiring of anonymity is the Scriptural method of living the Christian life. Any other method is purportedly of the Devil and doomed to an Armageddon destruction. Again quoting *The Watchtower* magazine, reading the May 1, 1957 issue, page 275:

> Being so closely associated with the mother organization, Christ's "bride" would certainly resemble her mother in all respects, as would even those Christians still on earth in the flesh who are engaged to be married to Christ. These would serve as her representatives and would therefore be easily recognizable by their conformity to God's requirements for his visible channel of communication.
>
> It becomes very clear that the so-called church organizations of Christendom could not be Zion's daughter organization. They hold no resemblance to God's woman organization in heaven. In their apostasy from true worship their "church" structures are not genuine nor apostolic, but are varied in form, some following the hierarchic structure, others being democratic or congregational and still others adopting the synodical type of church rule.
>
> All such forms are unauthorized and foster selfishness and self-centred ambition. Because they are not her children in fact, all of such counterfeit organizations wickedly oppose the "mother" of true Christians and thereby find themselves fighting against God and his king, Jesus Christ, who is the chief one in the universal organization of Jehovah.—Psalm 2.

You see, they believe that they are the "daughter" of a "mother" organization, and that God is the Father in said organization! They cannot be *individually* children of God, but only *organizationally*. The "daughter organization" is the "child" of the "mother organization". Everything is *organization!* The *individual* doesn't have a chance!

All this, of course, causes a change in a person's thinking. He is forced to give up being himself. He has to relinquish himself to the organization. He does not possess his own soul. He has sold out 100 per cent to the organization.

THE ANONYMOUS SON OF GOD

Right along this line of thinking, Jesus Christ, to them, is just another creature who has to await instructions from God to find out what He's supposed to do next!

The Watchtower magazine of November 1, 1957, page 660, discusses wisdom personified, as found in the eighth chapter of Proverbs. It is held by many that this refers to the Son of God. The article reads as follows:

This created Son of God did not then know that, long after Jehovah said to him: "Let us make man in our image," he himself would become a man that he might buy back mankind from the terrible consequences of the first man's unwisdom, his sinning against the simple command-ment of Jehovah God.

In other words, He did not know what God was going to do next! It was just one surprise after another! The idea of the above is, if the Son of God Himself was so ignorant and subject to the Father, look how ignorant *we* must be, and how much we should look up to the *organization!* I suppose the J. W.'s will assume that Jesus looked forward to periodic re-leases of "new truth" from the Father! I wonder who held the convention where the above-mentioned surprises was re-leased?

They take every opportunity to put Jesus Christ in his "place" within this "theocratic organization". Typical of such is this material found in *The Watchtower* magazine, July 15, 1959, page 421:

Certainly for one to believe the teachings of Christ he must know and worship the one God that Christ worshipped.

Do not erroneously conclude that Christians are to worship Christ; that is not what he taught. True, he is a god, a mighty one, but he did not worship himself and he did not teach his disciples to worship him....

It is true that his opponents accused Jesus of making himself equal to God by calling God his own Father, but in so doing they misrepresented the facts, as do those who teach the doctrine of the trinity today.

Please note: The above paragraph is in reference to John 5:18, which is an inspired record giving the conclusions, not of some mistaken Jews, but an apostle! But *The Watchtower* magazine of September 15, 1958, page 559, furthers its own delusion in these words:

Trinitarians may consider this a downgrading of the "Second Person of the Trinity", but if we accept the Scriptural testimony that Jesus was "the beginning of the creation by God," and "the firstborn of all creation," we will have no diffidence about applying to him the term archangel.

Jehovah's Witnesses are kept from historic Christianity by means of relinquishing their individuality and taking on anonymity; a puppet J. W. with the Watch Tower Society pulling the strings. Or, an automaton, whose actions are controlled by the manipulation of a certain mechanism.

ANONYMOUS PERSONS NOT SCHOLARS

As an excuse for the fact that the Watch Tower Society has but one Bible scholar (the vice president) and the remainder are NOT scholars, *The Watchtower* magazine of October 1, 1959 states on page 608:

So we let the literature speak for itself. The scholarliness of it, the logical presentation of the Scriptures that it sets forth and its faithful adherence to the Bible are things that should impress the reader and that should convince him that this is the Bible truth. Worldly scholarship is not the thing to be required....

With these things in mind, we encourage all who seek the Bible truth to see the prime necessity of the possession of the holy spirit on the part of those who are responsible for the material that goes into the publications of our Society. The evidence of the holy spirit in the quality and content of the writings published by the Watch Tower Society should be the thing that satisfies, that convinces, together with a comparison of these things with the inspired Word of God, the Holy Scriptures.

It is agreed that we should do that very thing. Only let it be known that we Christians reject the heretic teaching that the Spirit is an "active force" and accept the plain teaching of the Bible regarding the personality of the Holy Spirit. It is *that* kind of Holy Spirit that we look for evidence of, and shall use the Bible as our guide. Not tied to any earthly religious overlord, we are free as sons of God to receive the Holy Spirit, who will enable us to understand the Holy Word.

But the purpose of this chapter has not been completed. So we shall save our Scriptural investigation of doctrines for chapters that follow.

EFFECT OF GOVERNING BODY OF ANONYMOUS MEMBERS

Having lost the truth of the historic Christian faith, the Witnesses have also lost their individual right to become sons and daughters of God. It is only by a total renouncing of their former ways, and an embracing of their Saviour as their Lord and God that they will ever find freedom from the anonymity of the Watch Tower system of individual nothingness.

They believe that sinners devoid of the atoning blood can court favour with God. That is where the organization comes in. It replaces the need for the blood. It stands in stead and in place of Jesus Christ. It has removed Him from His position as Saviour and relegated Him to the level of a fellow creature, elevating the organization as the great theocratic saviour.

In effect, the organization acts as a sort of intercessor between the Witnesses and God. It accepts partial responsibility for their salvation. It has become a "Christ and the organization" arrangement.

All these are the various effects of anonymity on the minds of their people. It is a "theocratic organization" anonymity.

It is a phenomenon peculiar to itself, having no predecessor. It arose from the ranks of scepticism, as we have already shown. It was bred on the strength of an authority recognized as equal with the Bible; i.e., the organization. The organization has had to assume responsibility of pontifical authority. Disputers are considered heretics and cast out.

HOW ANONYMOUS ONES THINK

The effect all of this can have on a person's mind is startling. He no longer thinks of himself as a God-fearing individual (if he ever did). Suddenly, all piety and reverence has been removed from belief; all faith in the individual Christ has gone. It now becomes a matter of conducting and transacting business. It no longer involves worship (which is totally excluded). It has degenerated to a system of works and rewards.

It is typical modern organization procedure—big business. Businesslike methods are used for everything, and all is run on a production-line basis. All work for a salvation that never arrives or is attained. Figures and statistics are kept on everything. The amount of work performed is extolled worldwide. Percentage of increase is watched carefully. Those not producing sufficiently are removed from their position(s) of authority, or even purged.

God is viewed as an organization-god with a tally sheet covered with statistics and figures on business matters. He is never satisfied. Criticism of everything except the organization is encouraged. Everything else is mocked by them.

The method of practising Christianity to them is to become a "Jesus person". That is, you try and do the things Jesus did for the purpose of gaining your own salvation. They think that if Jesus had not "proven faithful" and done what God required of Him, He might have been left here on earth—no telling *what* would have become of Him! They are trying to do works similar to those performed by Jesus in order to "prove faithful" and "get everlasting life".

As we have seen from their publications, they believe it was the *life*, not the *death* of Jesus that really mattered. His death did nothing more than provide us with an opportunity to earn our own salvation. So it was really His obedient *life*, not the atoning blood that He shed, that saves. They further believe that without the pattern of His life to follow we would be lost. Yet their system of works is not based upon the New Testament at all, but on Old Testament law, etc. To them His death was only a means of putting an end to His life, the act by which He "gave up His body" to square Adam's disobedience. It mattered no more than that.

The blood is of no significance to them. The important thing is that He proved faithful *until* He expired. That qualified Him to be our example! So it is by following His *example* that we gain everlasting life, and NOT by means of His death, burial and resurrection.

WHOSE WILL BE DONE?

The Watch Tower thinking has led to where the Witnesses deify the organization until it can do no wrong. It developes a *present infallibility* on matters of faith and performance of works for salvation. Thus we have a GOVERNING PONTIFICAL HIERARCHY directing every movement of the organization and its members world-wide. The individual Witnesses have relinquished their own wills and are now governed by an organizational will.

The Witnesses believe they are doing "the divine will". But that must be imported Watch Tower-wise. It is the "divine will" as seen through the eyes of the Society. A God-directed will of the individual is excluded. That leaves only one will— that of the "governing body" of Jehovah's Witnesses, the Society itself!

The weight the Watch Tower Society carries with Jehovah's Witnesses is second to none. In a showdown between a disputed Bible passage (or text) and the Society, it is the Society who will always win. The Witnesses are so much more easily won over by the Watch Tower Society than by the Bible itself.

"THE FAITHFUL AND WISE SERVANT"

Jehovah's Witnesses believe that the Watch Tower Society is the *servant* of Matthew 24: 45, 46. The following is taken from Matthew Henry's *Commentary* on this subject; Volume V, page 364:

Now observe what Christ here saith, [1.] Concerning the *good servant*; he shows here what he is—*a ruler of the household*; what, being so, he should be—*faithful* and *wise*; and what, if he be so, he shall be eternally—*blessed*. Here are good instructions and encouragements to the ministers of Christ.

First, We have here his place and office. He is one *whom his Lord has made ruler over his household, to give them meat in due season.* Note,

1. The church of Christ is his household or family, standing in relation to him as the Father and Master of it. It is *the household of God*, a family named from Christ, Eph. 3:15.

2. Gospel ministers are appointed *rulers* in this household; not as princes (Christ has entered a caveat against that), but as stewards, or other subordinate officers; not as lords, but as guides; not to prescribe new ways, but to show and lead in the ways that Christ has appointed: that is the significant of the *hegoumenoi*, which we translate, *having rule over you* (Heb. 13:17); as *overseers*, not to cut out new work, but to direct in, and quicken to, the work which Christ has ordered; that is the significancation of *episkopoi* —*bishops*. They are the rulers by Christ; what power they have is derived from him, and none may take it from them, or abridge it to them....

3. The work of gospel ministers is to give Christ's household their meat in due season, as stewards, and therefore they have the keys delivered to them. (1.) Their work is to *give*, not to take to themselves (Ezek. 34:8)....

(2.) It is to give *meat*; not to give *law* (that is Christ's work), but to deliver those doctrines to the church which, if duly digested, will be nourishment to souls. They must give, not the poison of false doctrines, not the stones of hard and unprofitable doctrines, but the meat that is *sound* and *wholesome*.

This describes exactly what the Watch Tower Society is NOT doing! Further on Matthew Henry states, page 365:

He shall be preferred; *He shall make him ruler over all his goods.* The allusion is to the way of great men, who, if the stewards of their great house conduct themselves well in that place, commonly prefer them to be the managers of their estates.... But the greatest honour which the kindest master ever did to his most tried servants in this world, is nothing to that weight of glory which the Lord Jesus will confer upon his faithful watchful servants in the world to come.

The effect of anonymity on the mind has removed the understanding of this text from Jehovah's Witnesses. Thus they have become slaves of overlords who are making merchandise of them.

HOW DOES IT ALL HAPPEN?

This anonymity does not come all at once, of course. Many persons wonder exactly how the Watch Tower organization operates, and what it is that gets people so interested and involved in this work. The entire story will be given here to show you how it happens from start to finish. You who are now studying with them will see what is coming, and those of you on the fence will be able better to decide which side you would rather go over to.

Bear in mind that what now follows takes place usually within six months to one year. There are exceptions, of course. The effect of brainwashing is so thorough that people change entirely within this period of time. Usually, when a person is first contacted, it is by means of the

INITIAL HOUSE-TO-HOUSE-VISITING

The book *Qualified To Be Ministers* outlines for Jehovah's Witnesses the best methods to follow to successfully contact people and make them into Jehovah's Witnesses. We will use quotations from this book under each subject to show their standard procedures. Under "House-to-House Ministry" on page 175:

Now you approach the first door. How can a person introduce himself? He may state variously that he is a minister, a representative of the Watch Tower Society, one of Jehovah's Witnesses, doing an educational work, calling to encourage Bible study in the home, bringing good news, carrying out a public service, working with an international research group, bringing the people the good results of this research, working in conjunction with a world-wide society of ministers, working together with more than a half-million ministers, representing a New World Bible Society. In presenting the *New World Translation* one may say that he represents a Bible translating committee. During assemblies one may style himself a visiting delegate to the convention being held.

Now note the unique approach to persons who are unsuspecting of what is behind it all. Taken from page 176 of the above book:

> Obviously, your introduction must fit the person who answers your knock. If a man comes to the door, you can talk to him about things pertaining to the world situation, living standards, science, local events pertaining to business or civic interests, or anything concerning his family, its welfare and its safety. These things are of interest to man. Sometimes religion can be a subject, but more infrequently than with women.
>
> When a woman answers, religion is a good subject. Or her children, her household, the things that are going on locally, conditions among the local churches, living conditions, the cost of living, the new world and its beauties and wonders, prayer, all may be of interest to women.

But the J. W. has come to sell literature! How will he approach it? Reading from page 178 under the heading "Presentations":

> Having given your three-to-eight-minute sermon, then introduce the literature, showing the person how the publications go into detail on the subject you have talked about. Open the book or magazine to certain striking statements in its pages, to illustrations in the book or to chapter headings.

The purpose of all this is contained on page 179:

> Do not forget that our purpose is to help the people by getting the Kingdom literature into their hands, which they can read in their own homes and thus get a knowledge of God's purposes.

5

The purpose of this visit is to arouse interest and put literature into the hands of the listener. If this is accomplished there is a good chance that a return call will be made. These are called "back-calls", and the method of accomplishing them is found on page 207 of the above book, in the chapter titled

RETURN VISITS

In making a call back, we have a goal, a purpose. That is, to start a home Bible study eventually. The back-call itself is to improve the interest they already have, or to rekindle interest and clear out obstacles that stand in the way of their studying.

Now we read from this same chapter, page 209:

On a successful call, after having aroused further interest by turning to certain subjects in the book, or having cleared out obstacles by a Bible discussion, tell the person you want him to see in the publication he has what an abundance of good things God has for his people. Describe how greatly Jehovah's witnesses have helped honest seekers for truth by means of the literature.

These discussions are geared to last fifteen to twenty minutes, but they will stay for hours if permitted. These visits will continue until they have started a study in your home. This is the next step, found on page 211 of this book, titled

HOME BIBLE STUDIES

Ordinarily the study period will be about one hour. Often a chapter can be covered, but this depends on the aptitude of those studying. It is good to increase the pace of slow students gradually so that progress will be made. Stick to the lesson as closely as possible, and watch the time. Sometimes the householder will ask questions that do not pertain to the subject studied. Be kind and patient with such digressions.

If a question can be answered in a very few words, do so and say that you will give more information after the study. But do not let it overshadow and obscure the subject being studied. If the question is irrelevant, kindly ask the questioner to wait until the study is over and you will gladly take up the subject then. You may be able to show that this question will be answered in the next chapter, or in a few pages, and ask the group to wait until then and it will be cleared up.

One not-mentioned reason for the above statement is to make sure that the study conductor will not give an answer that might possibly contradict what the book says!

After a person has studied for awhile, he will then be directed to the organization itself. He will usually be taken to the area service centre, a home where a different book is being studied by a small group of Witnesses who meet there once a week. From there he will be directed to the Kingdom Hall. Here all the features of the organization are outlined to him.

From that point he is steered into the door-to-door work. Once he has joined the "theocratic ministry school" (the speech class) he will learn to give short talks before the audience. Door-to-door work is the next logical step. The method they use in handling this is covered in *Qualified To Be Ministers* on page 218, in the chapter titled

TRAINING NEW MINISTERS

The secret of success is, start training these new ones from the very earliest.... The great success of the missionary work in foreign lands is partly because of this.... So, take the new ones with you as early as possible. It is the "backbone" of our ministry.

This is good psychology (and this method should be adopted by our churches!) After accompanying a seasoned J.W. from door-to-door for a while, the new Witness will soon begin going to the homes by himself. When he runs into difficulties he will call on the mature Witness to help him out. There is but one step remaining now. It is

BAPTISM

He will be baptized by immersion, but not in the triune name. He is baptized in nobody's name at all. That is what officially makes him a "minister" and an official Jehovah's Witness! *That* is what they mean when they tell you they are ministers; namely, they have been baptized! The significance of the baptism to them is this: You give up your old life (whatever you were before) and begin a new life, dedicated (sins and all) to the service of Jehovah (in your unregenerate state). The age of the person does not determine whether or not he is "ordained". Men, women and children all fall into the same category. Splash!—and you are ordained!

As has been mentioned, an average conversion takes place within six months (to a year). The reason: Persistent follow-up by Jehovah's Witness. If it works for them as they are now, think what they could do if they were really *Christians*!

WHAT CAN WE DO?

That is what Christians everywhere ask me. They want to know what to do to help Jehovah's Witnesses, and lead them to Christ. The next chapter will begin to unfold that subject. You will see what Christians did for *me*, how *I* was helped, and how, as a result, I found Christ as my Saviour.

Several important points should be kept in mind when witnessing to the J. W.'s. You can see how they have been brainwashed, and the methods that were used on them to accomplish it. Plan your methods accordingly. Never fool or deceive them like the Watch Tower Society has done. Be honest and above board in everything. But most important of all—YOU MUST KNOW YOUR BIBLE AND KNOW IT WELL!

That is where the average Christian seems to fail. If you had made a systematic study of the Bible as the Witnesses have made a systematic study of their books, your knowledge would be superior to theirs. If Jehovah's Witnesses get you stuck, or if for any reason you cannot answer them on a subject under discussion, blame *yourself*! *They* are prepared! *You* are *not*!

Most of the time the Witnesses will call upon you when it is not convenient to talk with them. Ask them to come back, if you wish to deal with them. Do not pay for any literature they sell—you rob your own church if you do. Challenge them on the deity of Christ if a debate results, and stick to that subject from Genesis is Revelation. Do not waste time arguing about a multitude of doctrines that lead you nowhere. Get to the most important one of all and hold them to it.

Do not be discouraged if they appear to have refused the message of salvation. Pray for them. Remember—you may be the first Christian who has tried to witness to them in their lifetime. What you are telling them sounds new and strange to them, and requires patient, understanding and unhurried witnessing.

After you have sown the seed of God's Word be in earnest prayer for the one who has heard. You will have to use kindness and understanding all the way. Be firm, but polite. You will reap what you sow. Hatred begets hatred. Try love!

If you feel you cannot handle the Witness by yourself, call in other Christians to help you. You could spend your time in prayer while they are doing the witnessing.

Now it is time to give testimony as to how Christ changed me. I will tell how I reacted to the gospel and how the Watch Tower Society reacted to my reaction! This will be especially interesting to many Jehovah's Witnesses, because the Watch Tower Society (and many individuals in many places) has told one story, whereas the truth is *another*!

Let us go on now and pursue this subject; how *I* came face to face with the gospel.

6

I Come Face To Face With The Gospel

FACING THE PUBLIC

In those ten years that I spent as a Jehovah's Witness, I met all kinds of people. The religious folk indentified themselves in various ways. Some had the "live and let live" attitude— you could believe anything you wanted, and if you were satisfied, then it was the right thing, for *you* (not them). Others took a strict attitude about their church; you either had to be a member of *their* church or you could not be a real Christian (something like the Jehovah's Witness attitude!)

Four times in those ten years Christian people expressed enough interest in me to bring me into their homes and attempt to explain the gospel to me. The first three attempts were not real, serious, do-or-die attempts. But the fourth was, and continued for numerous meetings. This occurred in 1953. Also, often I would be doing street work on a Friday or Saturday night, and would be near one or more street corner meetings conducted by various evangelical groups. So I heard their message also. What were my reactions to all this?

I took notice of several things. For one, no one ever approached me from those street corner meetings to say a word about Christ. They seemed content to hand out their tracts and think they were preaching the gospel. Outside of this tract work they were quiet. If I attempted to start a conversation with them, they would refuse to talk! They seemed to be an ignorant sort of people. They did not appear to know the Bible very well. We Witnesses felt they were a minority, and that they could not talk about anything except Jesus and themselves, so it was best just to forget all about them! They never appeared very happy, or we detected a pseudo-happiness—a form of religious showmanship for the benefit of the public.

I had learned the doctrines taught by the Watch Tower Society as best I could. On certain occasions I would take another Witness along with me, whenever I was engaged in a discussion that looked as if it might get really involved. So I benefited both from my own personal study and from what I heard others say.

FACING CHURCH MEMBERS

I used to feel sorry for people who would say "I have my church." *I* had more than that! Even more to be pitied were those who could only say, "My minister takes care of that for me!" But to top it all would be for a man to come out and say, "My *wife* takes care of the religion in our family!" How pathetic and inane! It happened quite a few times.

It is odd how much importance people will place on trivial matters, but when it comes to God and the Bible they shrug it off, as if it did not matter at all. But even those who *did* indicate that they were Christians (not just mere church-goers) did not seem too willing to part with any information as to how *I might* become one of them. They seemed too interested in boasting about the fact that *they* were Christians!

Most church members, of course, represented themselves denominationally. By that I mean they would say, "I am a Baptist," or, "I am a Methodist" (or whatever else they happened to be). And so they were easily categorized. I, like all Jehovah's Witnesses, was always ready to argue *denomination*. We studied up on some of the teachings of various denominations, and got enough of each to argue about! Naturally, we tried to get people to agree with us as much as we could, but we always had to disprove their religion, or we would have been admitting that they were right and we were wrong!

Therefore I do not know exactly how many true Christians I met, because so few indicated such, or identified themselves sufficiently, so that at this time I could recall them. With all their preaching, few men ever came up to me and said that Jesus died to redeem me, so that I might spend eternity in heaven. And so I concluded there must be few indeed who believed that way!

No one had yet ever been successful in arguing me down on any Bibical doctrine. I was as staunch in my faith as I had ever been. And so it was at the age of twenty-four, I found myself a pioneer (local missionary) working in the East Falls section of Philadelphia. I was working in association with the Germantown Kingdom Hall. One reason I had chosen the territory where I was working—it had not been worked for two years, and it was a predominantly Catholic area. This presented a challenge—despite the fact that at least fifty per cent of Jehovah's Witnesses are former Catholics. I decided to work this territory and see what I could do, if anything.

My success surprised me. I was placing over 400 magazines a month, selling numerous books and Watchtower Bibles, and obtained quite a number of subscriptions for *The Watchtower* and *Awake!* magazines. I made back-calls and conducted studies. I stayed in this territory a number of months.

One day I was working a particular street that I had difficulty working. I suffer from "hay fever" and this street had just about everything growing on it that bothers us sufferers! I remember twice having to leave it, as this misery was afflicting me so badly. One day I made it through, and found myself, ultimately, at one particular house. The maid, who came once a week, answered. She listened to all I had to say, then turned and called the lady of the house. Since she left the door open, I walked in! When the lady came, I re-hashed my sales pitch all over again. She listened and explained what they were! Oh no! "Jesus-saved salvationists" again!

It happened that we had a discussion and I left a book free (she would not buy it). I received some Scriptures regarding salvation. I was not impressed. But I had been shown kindness and love. Most unusual! I made a return visit. I called on her and her husband. Received more Scriptures. I kept coming back, time and time again. At all times I was kindly received. Despite aggressiveness on my part, there was no hatred, no mockery, ridicule or scorn. This was part of the secret of their success. The other part was: They kept their mouth shut and the Bible open! Instead of giving their views, or even quoting Scriptures, they had me turn to various passages and read them out loud, and then asked for my explanation. Of course, I was trying hard to win them to the

Watch Tower view at all times. But they always seemed to have an answer from the Bible!

Six months after I had first knocked on their door, they made a suggestion: Since it was apparent that they could not fully convince me, would I be willing to come and converse on these matters with a couple men from their church? These men knew the Bible well, they told me. They would like me to discuss these matters with those men, while they merely listened. I agreed to come. Two down, and two to go! Would this never end?

I accepted the challenge. You see, I had always considered these "saved" people to be victims of a highly overworked imagination. They used expressions like, "I know Christ as my personal Saviour." That orbited over my head! What did they mean—*knowing* the Lord? What did they mean by *personal* Saviour? No one ever bothered to explain, so I concluded they did not know!

FACING THE GOSPEL

If they did not know what they were talking about, I could handle them! So on the night arranged, we met—I, the two men, and the two listeners. We started at eight o'clock and finished at one a.m. Five hours of rapid-fire debate. We did not lose a second's time. We used the Bible only, and stuck to one subject—the deity of Christ. If we had jumped from one subject to another, we would have accomplished nothing. We would have wasted all that time.

I felt that it was my duty to set them straight. They thought Christ was God! They really needed my help! Naturally, I was right and they were wrong! But somehow that night I failed to convince them of this. Of course, they had not convinced me of *their* way, either. So I was not worried.

It had appeared they were caught on John 1:1. The *New World Translation* reads: " ... the Word was a god." *That* should have settled it for everybody, but it didn't! So, in desperation I turned to the *appendix* that appeared in the back of *The New World Translation of the Christian Greek Scriptures*, and read what the translator(s) had put there to back up their translation. Here is what I read, from page 776:

In further proof that the omitting of the definite article

in the predicate of John 1:1 by the apostle was deliberately meant to show a difference, we quote what Dr. Robertson's *Grammar* says on page 767: "(i) NOUNS IN THE PREDICATE. These may have the article also."

Was I ever shocked when one of the men produced a copy of Robertson's *Grammar*! He then turned to the quotation above and continued to read from where they left off: "AS ALREADY EXPLAINED, THE ARTICLE IS NOT ESSENTIAL TO SPEECH". (That is, it could be either used or not used, without making any real difference). Now what was I going to do about *that*?

Nothing! What *could* I do? This was a tricky problem. I hadn't known matters were going to get this complicated. In our book studies we had been using *The Emphatic Diaglott* (a Greek-English interlinear translation, printed by the Watch Tower Society). We noticed that the word *theos* in the sentence "the Word was God" did not have the definite article *ho* before it; therefore we Witnesses concluded that the word was indefinite and meant "a god". Hence, the above material. Now if, as Robertson's *Grammar* stated, "the article is not essential to speech", the picture changed. Why had not the Watch Tower Society completed the quotation from the *Grammar*? It changed the idea altogether. However, I was no scholar (I had just found *that* out!), so I suggested that I would send this in to the Watch Tower Society, and as soon as I received an answer, I would bring it to the next meeting, or mail it in.

A month later the answer came. They said they were "inclined to answer, 'So what?' We still stick to what is said in the *New World Translation* appendix!" What an answer! How could I ever show *that* to him? How embarrassing! So the society had no answer for John 1:1! Well, well!

It had been decided that we would hold another meeting. This time the discussion was led by a new participant, a Christian business man well known in that area.* He permitted me to use the Watch Tower Bible; then promptly proceeded to prove to me from *it* that Jesus is Jehovah God the Son! We were reading Revelation 1:1, 17, 18; 21:6; 22:12-16. He asked me to read the verses slowly and carefully, then had

*Alex Dunlap, director of The Conversion Center, Havertown, Pennsylvania.

me concentrate on Revelation 1:8. Regarding that text he asked me. "*Does* it or does it *not* prove that Christ is God?"

I had never had to contend with the likes of *this* before! I wished I could get out of it. I could not. I sweated. *This* was the *Bible*! I could not deny what *it* said! Why should I? To remain a Jehovah's Witness, *that's* why! I was facing things I had never faced before. He was calling me to make a decision. I admitted that it did appear that the text says Christ is God. I decided I had enough of these meetings, and I quit.

FACING THE CHURCH

Before these people would let me go, however, they had me in church next Sunday morning! They knew I would not come back for another meeting. For six months this couple had been trying to get me to go to church with them. I would not go. Now we made a deal. I agreed to go to church if they would promise we would have no more meetings. They agreed and I went.

With them I attended a large, independent church just outside west Philadelphia. I first attended the adult men's Sunday School class. There, as a visitor, I introduced myself and mentioned what I was. I was laughed down for being a Jehovah's Witness. The men said all sorts of unkind things —like, "You don't even look like a Christian," etc. It was the type of treatment I had expected to get, and I was getting it! It looked like the Watch Tower Society was right after all, regarding what they said about these people! They were showing their true colours all right. This made me feel more sure than ever that I was doing right by remaining a Jehovah's Witness.

After this class I attended the main service of the morning. Of course, I listened with a chip on my shoulder. After that was over I was almost thrown out! In the midst of several belligerent arguments on my way out I recalled that the couple who had invited me into their home to hear the gospel had mentioned that they were praying for me. So, as I was leaving, I reminded the most persistent arguer that at least so-and-so had said they would *pray* for me. He said sneeringly, "O.K.—we'll pray for you!" What a way to end a service.

I walked from that church more determined than ever to

remain a Jehovah's Witness. On my way out the door I re-marked: "After hearing this, I'm glad I am a Jehovah's Wit-ness!" And I was. The kind couple who had started all this by arranging those meetings and I then parted; but not with a "good-bye". They would not say "good-bye", for I was to spend all eternity in heaven with them. Their last heartfelt words were, "We'll be praying for you!"

And so *that* was the climactic event of 1953 for me, rather than the huge covention Jehovah's Witnesses held at Yankee Stadium. These were the only "salvationists" who ever made a real effort to win me over. They had indeed succeeded far more than any others had, Yet, after that experience in church that Sunday, all that they had said seemed to be nullified. The way those church people acted seemed to belie the fact that they were Christians. Bear in mind, this treatment was not meted out by those who preached to me; but by others, members of the same church. However, I felt that what one member did reflected on all the others as well.

My final reactions to the entire episode was that I never wanted to see any of them again. I never intended to. Not only had they embarrassed me doctrinally, but their treat-ment of me (being what I expected it to be) satisfied me that I would be better off in the Kingdom Hall. I could certainly see that they knew the Bible (better than I did!), and that they would never be won over to the Watch Tower Society. And as for church—I felt that I had better stay in the organi-zation unless I wanted similar treatment all over again! So back to the organization I went, intending to stay! I say "back to", although I had never left it, of course. It's just that they had thought they could get me out of it, and in the pro-cess of those meetings believed they were influencing me away from the organization. It was sort of a testing-time for me, which I felt I came through successfully!

BUSINESS AS USUAL

I kept on in the pioneer work and continued having fairly good success. In 1955 I attended a large convention at Forbes Field in Pittsburgh, where I made a mental re-affirmation of my faith, becoming stronger than ever. I determined I would never speak against the Watch Tower Society. Apparently, those meetings had not worried me a bit! My faith was as strong as ever. It seemed, from all outward appearances, that it would always remain that way

But I made a recount of my life and experiences as a Jehovah's Witness. In the year that followed I continued on as usual (as I did for the next three and a half years) in the Witness work. There were some things that I could not see that did not satisfy me. Things I could see in others as well as myself. I realized we J. W.'s all shared a common fate —both present and future. We were all in original and personal sin—even our doctrine told us they were unremoved at this time. We hoped that we would die "faithful" (the degree of faithfulness was never set), and "come back" in the "new world". But it was only a "maybe" chance; we could never be sure.

Not only were all our sins unremoved, they were unforgiven. Now that does not bother some people. But at times it would bother me. I could see there was something lacking; something was needed that just was not there. Look how many people left the organization! Where did they go? What did they lose? What did they gain? Were they better off or worse off as a result as their having been among us? What else could a person turn to after leaving Jehovah's Witnesses? All else was supposed to be darkness—evil powers doomed to eternal damnation at Armageddon.

I could detect that everything we did as Jehovah's Witnesses —our door-to-door work, the studies, attending conventions, delivering lectures, yes, even *prayer*—was all to no avail. None of it ever seemed to reach God! It was all our *own* works, performed in sin.

Yet we simply *had* to believe that this was God's will for us; we dared not think otherwise. We had no alternative. It was either this or nothing. After all, it *was* logical! Everything fitted together so nicely. Of course, much of it was a constant repetition, but you had to take it as it came. I began to detect that the Society never had anything really new at all, but kept repeating over and over again, rephrasing and rehashing what I had been receiving since 1946.

THE NEW WORLD BIBLE TO THE RESCUE!

I was sold on the *New World Translation* right from the start. We received it at the first Yankee Stadium convention,

1950. It went like wildfire! I thought that we had the final answer now once for all. Our superficial study and investigation of it seemed to verify that.*

Certain "troublesome" texts were cleared up by the Watch Tower translation. Colossians 2:9 now read: "Because it is in him that all the fullness of the divine quality dwells for the body".† How fine! This fitted in very nicely with the "truth". It also suited Revelation 3:14 which (to us) taught that Christ was created: "These are the things the Amen says, the faithful and true witness, the beginning of the creation by God."

Another troublesome text was John 8:58 (if used with Exodus 3:14). Luckily the Watch Tower Bible now read: "Jesus said to them: 'Most truly I say to you, Before Abraham came into existence, I have been." How nice! Clears up the embarrassing difficulty previously existing. Settles it, once and forever!

Then, of course, there was Hebrews 1:8—"Thy throne, O God, is for ever and ever." That would never do! So our Bible now read: "God is your throne forever." Much better! More accurate! Just the way it should be! Nice, besides! They also took care of Titus 2:13 for us, making it read, "While we wait for the happy hope and glorious manifestation of the great God and our Saviour Christ Jesus", rather than "great God and Saviour of us, Christ Jesus" (*Emphatic Diaglott*). Saves a lot of embarrassment that way!

At John 20:28 Thomas said something he shouldn't have. At least, he could not be a Jehovah's Witness and get away with saying it! He called Christ his Lord and his God. But the Watch Tower Society still hasn't been able to translate *this* fact *away*!

The average Jehovah's Witness assumes that the translators of the *New World* Bible translating committee have done a good job with their translation. He puts himself in the place of these men, and imagines what *he* would do if he were in their place. He feels that *he* would be honest and give a proper translation, and so he feels that the Watch Tower leaders will do the same. That is where he makes a grave error! He

*The Society now has a new *Kingdom* edition of the Watchtower Bible, a Greek-English edition released at the conventions in 1969. It is more valuable than the first edition of 1950.

†Later changed when the revised edition was released in 1961.

78

has deified the leaders to where they can do no wrong, and so he puts blind trust in them.

FOR WHOM WAS THE BIBLE WRITTEN?

I had always believed the Bible to have the final word, but read it only through the eyes of Watch Tower material. We were told that the Bible was written only for the 144,000. Why so? Jehovah's Witnesses believe that only 144,000 people can go to heaven. They think the number was complete in 1931, and teach that only slightly over 10,000 of this number are still alive. However, the top directors of the Watch Tower Society are all of that number. They are the spiritual leaders of Jehovah's Witnesses, and, naturally, the correct interpreters of the Bible.

Now since they are the only ones who can properly interpret the Bible, the Bible was written for no one else. They believe it would be a closed book if it were not for the top ranking leaders of the Watch Tower Society. They believe that we have no individual right to the Bible, and aside from those Watch Tower leaders assigned to perform the task, it may not be interpreted. The other Witnesses may read it, but must go to the governing body for the interpretation. Non-J. W.'s may only get an understanding of the Bible by speaking to a Jehovah's Witness, because the J. W. has received *his* interpretation from the governing body! Thus, without the aid of materials produced by this group of spiritual leaders the Bible will remain a closed book.

I FACE THE "TRUTH" AS WELL AS THE BIBLE!

Now, what made my predicament unusual was that I had used my Watch Tower Bible in my series of discussions with the Christian people. And I still could not win! Somehow it had failed me! The text that got me (Revelation 1:8) read differently in the Watch Tower Bible, but that only added to the predicament. " 'I am the Alpha and the Omega,' says Jehovah God, 'the One who is and who was and who is coming, the Almighty'."

The reason for this difficulty was Revelation 22:12-16. The quotation marks beginning at verse 12 show one speaker right through to verse 16. In verse 13 He says: " 'I am the Alpha and the Omega, the first and the last, the beginning and the end'." Then, in verse 16, He says: "'I Jesus, sent my angel to bear witness to you people of these things for the congregations. I am the root and the offspring of David, and the bright and morning star'."

In verse 13 a marginal reference refers the reader to Isaiah 48:12, where we read: "Hearken unto me, O Jacob, and Israel my called: I am he; I am the first, I also am the last." THIS IS JEHOVAH GOD! Something was wrong, somewhere!

But where? THIS was not supposed to be the "truth"! It was supposed to be the other way around! I was backed into a corner by these passages in my own Bible. These things began to bother me during the years that followed those meetings in 1953.

Nobody had ever showed me these things before; how could I suddenly cope with them? The Watch Tower Society had never prepared me for arguments for use in cases like this! What did they expect the Witnesses to do in this type of situation? I had already asked the Society one question about the problem that puzzled me, concerning John 1:1, but they had made it clear they could not help me out. So I was left on my own, I knew, in this case. *Now* where was I to go for an answer?

I was not supposed to go anywhere else. The governing body of Jehovah's Witnesses was the only place I was to turn to for needed help. When *they* let you down, you were really sunk! The other Witnesses did not know anything. They could barely figure out the basic, elementary things! No use attempting to ask *them* difficult questions. Many of them would not even understand what I was talking about. I had found *that* out from personal experience! So I was forced to personally begin studying the Bible more thoroughly.

There I was: Stuck with two authorities that I felt I could rely on: the Bible, and the Watch Tower Society! The one had me confused, and the other had refused to straighten out that confusion! Now *there* was a fine predicament to be in!

I LOOKED FOR A FRIEND, BUT THERE WAS NO FRIEND

I tried speaking to some close friends about these matters, but that only made them suspicious of me, and they warned the local servants (leaders) to watch me closely! That did not help me any! What was I to do?

I had known for many years a certain J. W. who had a knowledge of Hebrew and Greek, plus a library of theological books. Witnesses like this are very few and far between! Especially *honest* ones! He and I had many discussions, and he helped me understand some of these perplexing problems. He was not satisfied either way on most of them. His attitude was, "Maybe there is and maybe there isn't; maybe it's so and maybe it isn't so." But at any rate he helped me get a basic, elementary grasp of things, including the Greek language.

It was not long before another blow was struck. One night in our Kingdom Hall I saw on a desk a copy of *Jehovah of the Watchtower.** I gave it a quick reading and decided to get a copy for myself, which I promptly did.

As a result, I wrote another letter to the Watch Tower Society, asking eight questions based on the *New World* Bible. These questions were a summary of points I got from this book. As of this date, I am too far removed from the time of that writing to remember exactly what those questions were. Perhaps I would have remembered if the Watch Tower Society had answered that letter! Never before in those ten years had they failed to answer any of my letters. But this one they did! Now, what under the sun was I supposed to do about THIS problem?

This kept getting more involved all the time, and the Society seemed to be up against something they could not get out of. I simply could not understand it. I never thought anything like this would happen. Yet it happened! Believe me, it was quite a blow to take! The only place to which I could turn for spiritual help had let me down. I was now left all on my own to fathom the problems for myself. And so I started to search the Bible even more, to see what it really did teach.

Soon thereafter I came across another book—*Thirty Years a Watchtower Slave*. This book planted a seed of suspicion in my mind that perhaps the Watch Tower Society was NOT "the faithful and wise servant" that they were supposed to be! What if they weren't?

Jehovah of the Watchtower, Martin and Klann, Zondervan. This book is now out of print.

6

I decided to take this book to my J. W. friend who knew Hebrew and Greek. I respected his opinion and wanted him to read it and tell me what he thought. His wife got very excited over this, and called her congregation servant (West Philadelphia unit) and my congregation servant (Germantown unit). Exactly what went on behind the scenes after that I do not know. But the result was: This woman's congregation servant told his people that I had been put on probation by the Society (limited activity basis), and was to be avoided! This occurred in 1956.

This meant I was supposed to be a deviationist and could not be trusted. Although this was a story made up for the occasion, most of those in the West Philadelphia unit suspected me, after that time. The man who started this rumour was a deliberate liar. He has acted as treasurer for the Watch Tower Society at certain large conventions, and so, in the eyes of many, is a trusted and respected Jehovah's Witness.

I noticed also, that about that time whatever I said was being listened to carefully in my own Kingdom Hall. Pressure began to be put on. I felt something was coming, but I did not know exactly what it would prove to be.

My conscience began to bother me. I had quit praying. What I had learned in over three years as a result of studying the Bible personally bothered me, too. For I had found the answer to the problem of the deity of Jesus Christ. It was a different one than the Society gave! I began to see that the Watch Tower Society and the Bible were at definite odds on certain important matters.

Then, too, Jehovah's Witnesses were beginning to show their true colours: liars, backbiters, etc. I saw that no one was allowed to study the Bible in their organization except through their books. The man who told the lie about my "probation" told my friend who helped me in my studies that all books not published by the Watch Tower Society were *trash*! That means that the Gilead library has over eight thousand volumes of *trash* in it! That means, also, that the Society quotes from trash in order to arrive at certain of their conclusions, which are based on publications other than those of the Society! This just goes to show how sold some of these Witnesses can get on the organization.

By this time we had reached the end of 1956. I turned in a

work report yet for January, 1957 and attended meetings into February. But a decision was about to be made.

A DEEP SEARCHING

But here I want to pause in my story. Why? Well, from 1953 through 1956 I engaged in a serious study of the Bible to settle the question once and for all as to the deity of Jesus Christ. I had naught else to turn to, and so I stayed with the Bible alone.

I could hardly believe what I was reading. I did not expect it to be that way. It was not supposed to be! But two opposite teachings could not *both* be true; if the Watch Tower Society was right the Bible was wrong. They were supposed to be in agreement. Were they?

That is what I will go into next. I want to outline for you the struggle that went on while I was endeavouring to find the real truth from God's Word. It was not easy. I did not know then what I know now. If I had only known at the age of seventeen what I know now, I never would have become a Jehovah's Witness!

The best defence against this heresy is a knowledge of the Bible. Knowing it you will never be swayed. The more I learned of the Bible, the more I could see the fallacy of the Watch Tower teachings. The Bible became a different book to me when I began to read it without the Watch Tower teachings to influence me.

And so I will tell you now how my conscience struggled against my mind, after I learned the real truth from the Bible. Then I will tell you how I was fully converted. But first things first. I have already told you *why* I started, what I concluded, and what I did about my conclusions. Later I will tell you what the Watch Tower Society did about my conclusions! But now, here is the story of the struggle that ensued as a result of my hearing the gospel of the Lord Jesus Christ.

7

The Struggle That Ensued As A Result

MY IMMEDIATE REACTION

After the 1953 series of meetings had taken place and I went my way, there were three things that would not leave my mind: (1) Revelation 1:8; 22:12-16 indicated that Christ is God; (2) The *New World Translation* of John 1:1 was possibly wrong; (3) I read the Bible improperly—through "Jehovah's Witnesses glasses".

I had been learning only *one* thing from the Bible; and now this happened, and I learned something else! Only I was not supposed to learn anything *else* from the Bible! But after sending in eight questions regarding the Watch Tower Bible and receiving no answer, I knew then that if I ever got answers to these questions it would be as a result of my own personal study of the Scriptures.

I had never done anything like this prior to 1953. It had not been necessary, for the Society had always taken care of that for me! Now I found it necessary to think for myself. I was alone with the Bible—no outside influences to colour my thinking. I decided to begin a study that would give me the final answer as to whether or not Jesus was truly God.

THE SEARCH BEGINS

The best way to begin, I thought, would be to look up various texts in numerous translations of the Bible, and see if they differed greatly. I would stick to the subject of the deity of Christ until I had it proved one way or the other. To begin, I tackled John 1:1. Here is the way it reads in the left-hand column in *The Emphatic Diaglott*, a Society-printed

Greek interlinear translation made by Benjamin Wilson, a newspaper editor who taught himself Greek, and which uses the Griesbach text:

EN ARCHE EN HO LOGOS KAI HO LOGOS EN PROS TON THEON KAI THEOS EN HO LOGOS. "In beginning was the Word and the Word was with the God and a god was the Word".

The Biblically-illiterate Witnesses used to point out that there are TWO different words used for *God—theon* and *theos*—and claimed that this proved that two different *gods* were spoken of here. These words both mean "God". In fact, they are merely different grammatical forms of the same Greek word. See Harper's *Analytical Greek Lexicon,* pages 193, 194.

Later the Witnesses came to stress the fact that *theos* sometimes appears *with* the article and sometimes *without.* This is supposed to distinguish the supreme God, Jehovah, from any lesser god, such as Christ, the Logos or Word. But do grammarians agree? I shall here limit myself to only one. Quoting *A Critical Lexicon and Concordance to the Greek New Testament* by E. W. Bullinger (1957) we read on page 331:

1. *Theos,* God. A name reclaimed from the heathen, and used in N. T. for the true God. . . . *Theos* however, having lost the meaning of the one God came to mean "a God" only, one of the many gods. Hence it became necessary in [the] N. T., generally, to distinguish it by the article, *ho theos,* the one supreme with whom is the fountain of life and light. . . .

Further down, on the same page, we read:

In the following references (*distinguished by the asterick*), *Theos* is used without the article, and denotes the conception of God, as an Infinite and perfect Being, one who is almighty, infinite, etc.

Bullinger then gives a list of numerous New Testament references in which *Theos* without the article is used with reference to God, the Infinite and Almighty. JOHN 1.1 is INCLUDED IN THIS CATEGORY!

In *The Emphatic Diaglott* itself, Mr. Wilson was honest enough to translate it the correct way in his right-hand column. There it reads: "In the beginning was the Logos, and the Logos was with God, and the Logos was God."

So that throughout John 1:1 was proving the "a god" theory! The men (or *man*?) who translated the Watch Tower Bible obviously knew all this at the time of translation.

THE SEARCH DEEPENS

This was really beginning to bother me now! So "the Word was God" after all! Well, if so, the entire New Testament would back it up. So I decided to find all I could find. Searching further, I went to Revelation 1:8, a text that had gotten me started in all this in the first place, when compared with Revelation 22:12-16. It caused me to see that the "Alpha and Omega" was both Jehovah God and Jesus Christ!

Reading on in Revelation chapter one, I came to verses 17 and 18 (reading now the A.S.V.): "And when I saw him, I fell at his feet as one dead. And he laid his right hand upon me, saying, Fear not; I am the First and the Last, and the Living one; and I was dead, and behold, I am alive for evermore, and I have the keys of death and of Hades." Certain Witnesses insisted that only Jehovah was truly "the first and the last" (Isaiah 44:6), and that Jesus really meant "first-born" here rather than "the first and the last". They claimed that this is what the "original Greek" says. So what *does* the Greek say?

The word *protos* means "first", and *prototokos* means "first-born". The text in question reads: EGO EIMI HO PROTOS KAI HO ESCHATOS. So it really says "the first and and the last" after all! This same title appears at Revelation 2:8 (*A.S.V.*): "These things saith the first and the last (HO PROTOS KAI HO ESCHATOS), who was dead, and lived again." Again, without dispute, this spoke of Jesus Christ! Only a most illogical person would say there are two "firsts" and two "lasts", in an attempt to weaken Christ's claim.

At Revelation 21:6 Jehovah the Father says: "I am the Alpha and the Omega, the beginning and the end." This is the same as He is called at Revelation 1:8. That puts us in touch with chapter twenty-two, verse 13: "I am the Alpha and the Omega, the first and the last, the beginning and the end." But who is speaking here? At verse 16 you see that it is JESUS speaking!

Unpleasant facts, maybe, when you are a Jehovah's Witness, but it is the Bible; can you rightly reject it? I struggled with what I was seeing. It was not supposed to be that way! But it was! Now what was I supposed to do? Go on with the study!

Colossians 2:9 would be the next logical step. What did it *really* say? The Greek text reads: HOTI EN AUTO KATOIKEI PAN TO PLEROMA TES THEOTETOS SOMATIKOS. That was not the way *it* was supposed to be, either! Why not? Here is the word-for-word literal translation in English: BECAUSE IN HIM DWELLS ALL THE FULLNESS OF GODHEAD BODILY. My Watch Tower Bible read: "Because it is in him that all the fullness of the divine quality dwells for the body." (The 1961 revised edition now reads: "Because it is in him that all the fullness of the divine quality dwells bodily.") Checking other translations of this text, you find:

"For it is in him that all the fulness of the Deity dwells bodily" (Moffatt, 1901). "It is in Christ that the entire Fulness of deity has settled bodily" (Moffatt, 1935). "Because in him dwells all the Fullness of the Deity bodily" (*Emphatic Diaglott*). "For it is in Christ that the complete being of the Godhead dwells embodied" (*New English Bible*). "For in Him all the fulness of the Godhead dwells bodily" (The Berkeley Version). Once again, the *New World* translators are trying to pull a fast one.

THE PLOT THICKENS!

What a revelation this was beginning to become! I felt encouraged to go on. Something was going to come of this, although I did not know *what*. There was much more yet to be found, so I decided to go on and find it.

What about Thomas and what he called Jesus? This is recorded at John 20:28. There Thomas, who had doubted that the Lord had risen, now speaks to him and says: HO KURIOS MOU KAI HO THEOS MOU. This comes out word-for-word in literal English, THE LORD OF ME AND THE GOD OF ME. Most translations simply read, "My Lord and my God". Surely these are words of worship!

When the angel in Revelation was worshipped, he prohibited it, saying: "No, not that! I am but a fellow-servant with you and your brothers who bear the testimony to Jesus. It is God you must worship" (Revelation 19:10; 22:9; *New English Bible*). Therefore Jesus, who did not rebuke Thomas, must have been *higher* than an angel!

Notice in the above Greek text that Jesus is called *ho theos*, that is, *theos* with the definite article! That is what the Father calls Jesus at Hebrews 1:8, where we read, "Thy throne, O God, is forever and ever." The Greek text reads not merely "O God", but *ho theos* again—*the* God! I suppose the Father should know who Jesus Christ is!

This was really becoming involved now! All the while my study was going on (for over three years) I went out in the Witness work as usual. Now my view was being broadened. Slowly I felt a release coming—slowly but surely. But one does not suddenly break off from an organization held to be "God's organization". You must tread carefully lest you turn your back on Jehovah God!

But the story is far from being over. Look at John 5:18, for example. Read the context carefully. The conclusion reached in verse 18 is NOT that of the Jews, but of John! He says that Jesus' declaration of His deity is what angered the Jews, besides His breaking the sabbath.

Now I found something in the Old Testament that shocked me. It is found at Isaiah 9:6, where the Messiah is spoken of in these words: "His name shall be called Wonderful, Counsellor, the Mighty God, the everlasting Father, the Prince of Peace." In Hebrew the title "mighty God" is EL GIBBOR. It means "God the mighty", and is rightly translated into English as "the mighty God". This is the title of Jehovah God at Isaiah 10:21 and Jeremiah 32:18. Were there *two* "mighty Gods"? That would be polytheism!

WHAT THE SEARCH REVEALED

I found that there is but one God, and that He is revealed in the Old Testament as Jehovah; in the New Testament as Jesus (Jehovah the Son). This was very anti-Watch Tower! Actually, I did not know what to do. I decided to continue my study until I could really be sure. After I was sure beyond the shadow of a doubt, then I would act.

You see, being so tightly tied to the organization, it was not easy to break away from it. I thought as did all the others, that this was *God's* organization, and wanted to be careful how I reacted to what I now saw in the Bible. If there was a way of reconciliation, I wanted to find it. I wanted to see if it was at all possible to believe as I did now about Christ and still remain in the organization. I soon found out that it was impossible!

I saw that you could not be a Jehovah's Witness with mental reservations of your own. It was either all or nothing. You could not view things more broadly than the Society would allow. You had to maintain their narrow-minded, bigoted way of thinking or leave. That made this matter all the more complicated. I was stuck to teaching the Society's way of thinking at the homes of people, when I had differences of opinion myself. What could I do? I did nothing for the moment. I just bided time and continued to preach as a Witness.

THE OTHER SIDE OF THE STORY

I now saw two sides to this story about Jesus Christ. What about the other side—the one I had originally held? How could I accept that along with what I knew now? I decided I would reject the erroneous texts in the *New World Translation* wherever I might find them. As to the true teaching that Christ was also a man, I would investigate that a little more carefully than I had done before. How could I reconcile the two teachings? No easy task, this!

There was that text most commonly used to "prove" that Jesus was created—Revelation 3:14, which reads: "These things saith the Amen, the faithful and true witness, the beginning of the creation of God." Moffatt's 1901 translation reads: "These things saith the Amen, the faithful and true witness, the origin of God's creation." So reads also Williams and Goodspeed. Farrar Fenton has it, "The Beginner of God's creation." *The New English Bible* (published in 1961) reads "The prime source of all God's creation."

This text must harmonize with John 1:3, which reads: "All things were made through him; and without him was not anything made that hath been made." Does this mean that Jesus made Himself? Absurd. Does creation exclude Him? Evidently! Either that or we have a created Creator!

So evidently then, Revelation 3:14 identifies Christ as the one who *began* the creation.

The Greek word ARCHE is used, and carries various translations. It does NOT mean "beginning" here in the sense that Christ Himself *began*. But rather, that He caused creation to begin by beginning it. "In the beginning the word WAS ..." He did not Himself begin with the "beginning".

What about Colossians 1:15, where we read regarding Christ: "Who is the image of the invisible God, the firstborn of all creation" *A.S.V.*)? Doesn't *firstborn* mean He was created? In Greek *firstborn* is *prototokos*. If it meant *first-created* it would be *protoktiseos*. This word *prototokos* occurs eight times throughout the New Testament. At no place does it indicate *creation*. Jesus is not an object of His own or His Father's creation. Therefore He could not be the "firstborn" of creation in the sense that He is part of it. *The New English Bible* renders Colossians 1:15: "He is the image of the invisible God; his is the primacy over all created things."

Then there is Proverbs 8:22. Jehovah's Witnesses have always taken the text to indicate that Christ was created. It reads: "Jehovah possessed me in the beginning of his way, before his works of old." The best you can find as a result of reading the chapter is that it is Wisdom that is spoken of. To the Greeks wisdom was *logos*—eloquence, thought, expression, intelligence, etc. It is thought by some that the Son of God is the Wisdom of God, that is, the *Logos* of God. If so, then if there was a time when the Son did not exist, then there was a time when God was without wisdom!

Although the *New World Translation* of this portion of the Bible had not come out yet when I was wrestling with this problem, I will quote their version of Proverbs 8:22 to show their deceitful translation: "Jehovah himself produced me as the beginning of his way, the earliest of his achievements of long ago." They translate the Hebrew word *qanah* as "produced". They have attached the meaning of another Hebrew word, *qarab* here. The average J. W. reader is thus deceived. They have deified the Society to where it makes no errors, and they would never suspect it of doing anything like this!

So it is quite evident that Proverbs 8:22 does NOT prove the "creation" of the Son of God, either!

WHAT ABOUT JESUS' "INFERIORITY"?

What about Jesus' statement "My Father is greater than I"

(John 14:28)? He said that BEFORE His resurrection—not after! There is a difference. This is not an eternal condition; it is only applied while Jesus was in the flesh as a man, devoid of His heavenly glory. We see where Jesus prayed for JEHOVAH'S GLORY to be restored to Him: "And now, Father, glorify thou me with thine own self with the glory which I had with thee before the world was" (John 17:5, A.S.V.). We are reminded of God's words at Isaiah 42:8. "I am Jehovah, that is my name; and my glory will I not give to another." Yet Jesus prayed for that glory to be RESTORED to Him! That is, the GLORY OF THE FATHER RESTORED TO THE SON! We never learned *that* in the Kingdom Hall!

What about Philippians 2:5-8? The Watch Tower Society uses this passage to "prove" that Jesus was less than Jehovah the Father, and hence inferior. We read: "Have this mind in you, which was also in Christ Jesus: who, existing in the form of God, counted not the being on an equality with God a thing to be grasped, but emptied himself, taking the form of a servant, becoming in the likeness of men; and being found as a man, he humbled himself, becoming obedient unto death yea, the death of the cross" (A.S.V.). *The New English Bible* translation of this passage is noteworthy:

> Let your bearing towards one another arise out of your life in Christ Jesus. For the divine nature was his from the first; yet he did not prize his equality with God, but made himself nothing, assuming the nature of a slave. Bearing the human likeness, revealed in human shape, he humbled himself, and in obedience accepted death—death on a cross.

It might be well for us to consider the entire context, running from verse five to verse ten. An excellent consideration of this passage is found in Matthew Henry's *Commentary*, Volume VI, page 733:

> 1. Here are the two natures of Christ: his divine nature and his human nature. (1.) Here is the divine nature: *Who being in the form of God* (v. 6), partaking of the divine nature, as the eternal and only begotten Son of God ... it is of the same import with being the *image of the invisible God* (Col. 1:15), and the *brightness of his glory*, and *express image of his person*, Heb. 1:3.

He thought it not robbery to be equal with God; did not think himself guilty of any invasion of what did not belong to him, or assuming another's right. He said, *I and my Father are one,* John 10:30. It is the highest degree of robbery for any mere man or mere creature to pretend to be equal with God, profess himself *one with the Father.* This is for man to rob God, not in tithes and offerings, but of the rights of his Godhead, Mal. 3:8.

And he thought it not robbery to be equal with God; he did not greedily *catch at,* nor covet and affect to appear in that glory; he laid aside the majority of his appearance while he was here on earth, which is supposed to be the sense of the peculiar expression *ouk harpagmon hegesato.*

(2.) His human nature: He was *made in the likeness of men,* and *found in fashion as a man.* He was really and truly man, *took part of our flesh and blood,* appeared in the nature and habit of man. And he voluntarily assumed human nature; it was his own act, and by his own consent. We cannot say that our participation of the human nature is so. Herein he *emptied himself,* divested himself of the honours and glories of the upper world, and of his former appearance, to clothe himself with the rags of human nature. *He was in all things like to us,* Heb. 2:17.

2. Here are his two estates, of humiliation and exaltation. (1.) His estate of humilitation. He not only took upon him the likeness and fashion of a man, but the *form of a servant,* that is, a man of mean estate. He was not only God's servant that He had chosen, but He came to minister to men, and was among them as one who serveth in a mean and servile state.

One would think that the Lord Jesus, if he would be a man, should have been a prince, and appeared in splendour. But quite the contrary: *He took upon him the form of a servant.* He was brought up meanly, probably working with his supposed father at his trade. His whole life was a life of humiliation, meanness, poverty, and disgrace; he had nowhere to lay his head, lived upon alms, was a *man of sorrows and acquainted with grief,* did not appear with external pomp, or any marks of distinction of other men. This was the humiliation of his life.

But the lowest step of his humiliation was his dying the death of the cross. *He became obedient to death, even the death of the cross.* He not only suffered, but was actually and voluntarily obedient; he obeyed the law which he brought himself under as Mediator, and by which he was obliged to die....

There is an emphasis laid upon the manner of his dying, which had in it all the circumstances possible which are humbling: *Even the death of the cross,* a cursed, painful, and shameful death,—a death accursed by the law (*Cursed is he that hangeth on a tree*)—full of pain, the body nailed through the nervous parts (the hands and the feet) and hanging with all its weight upon the cross,—and the death of a malefactor and a slave, not of a free man,—exposed as a public spectacle. Such was the condescension of the blessed Jesus.

(2.) His exaltation: *Wherefore God also hath highly exalted him.* His exaltation was the reward of his humiliation. Because he humbled himself, God exalted him; and he *highly exalted him, huperupsose,* raised him to an exceeding height. He exalted his whole person, the human as well as the divine; for he is spoken of as being in the form of God as well as in the fashion of man.

As it respects the divine nature, it could only be the recognizing of his rights, or the display and appearance of the *glory he had with the Father before the world was* (John 17:5), not any new acquisition of glory; and so the Father himself is said to be exalted. But the proper exaltation was of his human nature, which alone seems to be capable of it, though in conjunction with the divine.

His exaltation here is made to consist in honour and power. In honour, so *he had a name above every name,* a title of dignity above all the creatures, men and angels. And in power: *Every knee must bow to him.* The whole creation must be in subjection to him: *things in heaven, and things in earth, and things under the earth,* the inhabitants of heaven and earth, the living and the dead.

At the name of Jesus; not at the sound of the word, but the authority of Jesus; all should pay a solemn homage. And that *every tongue should confess that Jesus Christ is Lord*—every nation and language should publicly own the universal empire of the exalted Redeemer, and that *all power in heaven and earth is given to him,* Matt. 28:18. Observe the vast extent of the kingdom of Christ; it reaches to heaven and earth, and to all the creatures in each, to angels as well as men, and to the dead as well as the living.—*To the glory of God the Father.* Observe, It is to the glory of God the Father to confess that Jesus Christ is Lord; for it is his will that *all men should honour the Son as they honour the Father*, John 5:23. Whatever respect is paid to Christ rebounds to the honour of the Father. *He who receiveth me receiveth him that sent me*, Matt. 10:40.

THE FATHER AND SON EQUAL?

Jesus receives the title of God everywhere in the New Testament. At Titus 2:13 He is called MEGALOU THEOU KAI SOTEROS HEMON CHRISTOU IESOU, that is, GREAT GOD AND SAVIOUR OF US, CHRIST JESUS. At Titus 1:4 we read of "God our Saviour", and in verse 5 of "Christ Jesus our Saviour". So here He is God the Saviour!

Regarding Him 1 John 5:20 says, "This is the true God." That is hard to get away from! Either He is or He isn't. There are no two ways about it. I had to accept one and reject the other. It was not an easy thing to do. It is not easy for anyone to do.

Jehovah's Witnesses use John 5:19 as a text supposedly proving that Jesus is not equal to the Father. However, notice how it back-fires on them: "Jesus therefore answered and said unto them, Verily, verily, I say unto you, the Son can do nothing of himself, but what he seeth the Father doing: FOR WHAT THINGS HE DOETH, THESE THE SON ALSO DOETH IN LIKE MANNER."

Stop and think: If he were but a man, how could He *see* the Father doing *anything*? It says that whatever the Father does the Son also does IN LIKE MANNER. How could He if He was inferior to the Father? This text proves equality, for the Son duplicates all that the Father does.

The Watch Tower Society teaches that Jesus became the Messiah at the age of thirty (the old heresy of "adoptionism"), when He was baptized. The Bible teaches otherwise. At Luke 2:11 we read: "For there is born to you this day in the city of David a Saviour, who is Christ the Lord" (*A.S.V.*). The word IS is translated from the Greek word *esti*. *Christ* is Greek for "Messiah". So the Bible teaches that at birth Jesus was the Messiah. We also read of how the angels were called by

God the Father to worship Jesus at His birth. This is found at Hebrews 1:6: "When he bringeth in the firstborn into the inhabited earth he saith, And let all the angels of God worship him."

The Watch Tower Society also teaches that Jesus is actually Michael the archangel. Yet the Bible tells us at Hebrews 1:5: "For unto which of the angels said he at any time, Thou art my Son, This day have I begotten thee? and again, I will be to him a Father, and he shall be to me a Son?" The obvious answer is, to NONE of them—Michael included! Further, Hebrews 2:5 reminds us, "For not unto angels did he subject the inhabited earth "

The evidence is overwhelming! But—could it be that *God's organization* is wrong? Maybe it will pay to take another look as to whether or not this *is* God's organization! If it *is*, it will certainly back up what the Bible teaches! But alas; the Bible is supposed to back up what *it* says. Sad, but true.

DID GOD DIE?

That is the problem Jehovah's Witnesses face when confronted with the deity of Christ. It takes an understanding of the two natures of Jesus to understand this. It must be understood that God was in Christ, reconciling the world unto Himself. If an effort is not made to understand this, you are permitting Satan to keep you blinfolded to the truth.

Jehovah's Witnesses shrug off the problem by saying, "No man has seen God at any time" (John 1:18). But Scriptures compare with Scriptures. And so we read Jesus' words at John 6:46, quoting *The New English Bible*: "I do not mean that anyone has seen the Father. He who has come from God has seen the Father, and he alone." Then reading John 14:9: "Anyone who has seen me has seen the Father." Jehovah's Witnesses counter with, "Oh, that means they saw the *attributes* of the Father in the Son!" They forget that Jesus said, "Do you not believe that I am in the Father, and the Father in me?" (John 14:10). Jesus was as much IN THE FATHER as the Father was IN THE SON.

There was a mystical union between the Father and the Son that is unexplainable. Jesus said, "He that beholdeth me beholdeth him that sent me" (John 12:45). Weymouth's translation reads, "He who sees me sees Him who sent me." Did they or did they not? What does the Bible say? At John 13:20 we read: "He that receiveth me receiveth him that sent me."

Jehovah's Witnesses raise the question, "To whom did Jesus pray on the cross, if He was God?" Also, regarding His baptism, "Whose voice came from heaven? Jesus' own voice?" They have not been able to distinguish between God the Father and God the Son. Therein lies their difficulty. As to *how* the two can be equal, and yet be separate and both the one God yet not the same Person, this is not *explained* in the Bible. But it is *taught*. I was content to accept it on the assumption that God ought to know who He Himself is, and that satisfied me.

This much I knew: The Bible teaches that Christ is God— and that was good enough for me. Who was I to argue back? Why should I even dare to think to do such a thing? Who gave me a right to argue back to God? My pride must bend; my will must bow; my soul must yield.

WHAT ABOUT SALVATION?

Tied in with the deity of Christ was His Saviourhood. I had to figure out just what rôle Jesus played in my salvation. In ecclesiastical circles today this study is known as *soteriology*. Jesus had never been more than a "big brother" who was an underling of God just as I was. Now with *this* viewpoint of Him, just learned from the Scriptures, how was I to view Him as Saviour? Did His deity change matters any? Apparently it did. And so I began to do what I could to find out what His being my Saviour meant, if anything. This was not easy, either!

As far as I could detect, the story of the blood shed at Calvary for my sins seemed to answer the problem of salvation. But how? I could not say that I knew I was *unsaved*, as I did not know what it was to *be* saved! But I knew I was in the same position as all other Witnesses. No miracle had ever occurred in my life to remove either original sin or my own personal sins against God. I was in the same boat with all the other Witnesses.

But yet, somehow, I knew there was something personal connected with Christ's death; something that involved *me— personally*. To what extent I did not know. All I knew was that Christ was the Saviour, and He is God the Son. I could not explain it, and I made no attempt to.

Naturally, all of this I had to keep to myself, outside of a couple close, personal friends that I could confide in. This made it even more of a struggle. I could see what kind of an organization it *really* was; it certainly was not very pleasing to the Lord—*that* I knew! But I could not leave—not yet.

ENTER THE HOLY SPIRIT

So far I have not mentioned the Holy Spirit. This adds on to the subject of the deity of Christ, making a trinity. I had to face *this* problem, also. I certainly could not avoid it! I made no effort to. I decided I would investigate *this,* also. So I did.

I concluded that if the deity of Christ were NOT the laughing matter Jehovah's Witnesses made it to be, then perhaps the trinity wasn't either. Remember—I did not know the Bible *then* as I know it *now.* I am endeavouring to show you what I learned *then,* not what I have learned *since* then. Later in the book I shall deal more fully with the deity of Christ and the Trinity. But now let us proceed to what I endeavoured to find out about the Holy Spirit.

It was plain that the Bible indicated there was more to the Holy Spirit than the Watch Tower Society allowed for. I had denied His *personal* existence for many years, as I did the deity of Christ. Slowly but surely, however, the truth unfolded as I read the Bible.

At John 14:26; 16:13, 14 we read from *The New English Bible*:

> But your Advocate, the Holy Spirit whom the Father will send in my name, will teach you everything, and will call to mind all that I have told you. However, when he comes who is the Spirit of truth, he will guide you into all truth; for he will not speak on his own authority, but will tell only what he hears; and he will make known to you what he hears; and he will make known to you the things that are coming.

Then, the following verse adds:

> He will glorify me, for everything that he makes known to you he will draw from what is mine.

7

Read this from any translation of the Bible you wish; it is essentially the same in them all. These words describe acts that only a *person* could perform.

Again, we read at John 15:26 (*A.S.V.*): "But when the Comforter is come, whom I will send unto you from the Father, even the Spirit of truth, which proceedeth from the Father, he shall bear witness of me." At Revelation 22:17 we read: "And the Spirit and the bride say, Come." All these texts denote *personality*. Notice—the Holy Spirit, a *he*, not an *it*, teaches; brings to mind; guides into truth; speaks; hears; declares future things, glorifies; comforts; bears witness, and *comes*, as a *person* comes.

The Holy Spirit takes the place of a person, namely, Jesus Christ. Could an "active force" do all that Jesus did and then come? If so, then Jesus was not a real person, but only a force! At Ephesians 4:30 we see that the Holy Spirit can be *grieved*. How could you possible grieve a mere force?

These facts moved me deeply. It was plain that there was much more to it than the Watch Tower Society allowed for. This was *God's* Word, and the Watch Tower was *man's* word. I knew which side I was on!

But yet I hesitated. Almost ten years had elapsed now since I had become a Witness. Would I turn my back upon it all, just like that? Where would I go from here? Where *is* there to go? Out into the world? What of the coming judgment? Oh, I know; the Society says there is not going to be that kind of a judgment, but suppose they are wrong—what then? After all, Hebrews 9:27 *does* say, "And inasmuch as it is laid up for men once to die, and after this the judgment . . ." Suppose the Watch Tower Society is wrong, and this verse means what it says, literally? Yes; what then?

JEHOVAH'S WITNESS REACTION

Towards the end of 1956, I gradually put in less and less time in the door-to-door work. I had a difficult time conducting the book study I had, knowing that I hardly agreed with the Society any longer. I did not feel like going from door-to-door and telling people things I was no longer sure of myself.

I spoke to a couple of close friends one day in their home about the trinity. What a furor it raised! I never brought *that* up again! It was at this time that the congregation servant of the west Philadelphia Kingdom Hall lied and said that I had been put on probation. It was then, also, that my own congregation servant kept a wary eye on me. Some of the Witnesses were talking about my suspicious attitude towards certain things. My friend who knew Greek and Hebrew told me I could be disfellowshipped in my present position. He himself did not swallow half of the Watch Tower doctrines, but remained a Witness for other reasons.

1956 ended. I hardly had the heart to start a new year as a Jehovah's Witness! I did manage to put forth a feeble effort. I had ceased answering questions in the "Watchtower study". I simply could not bring myself around to it. There was too much in those publications that did not square with the Bible as it should. There was entirely too much wrong for the whole thing to be right.

But there wasn't anyone to go to and ask for advice. By now most of my friends ignored me. They detected a deviation from the "party line". A couple of times some friends asked me if I had been disfellowshipped. Only God knew exactly what rumours they were spreading, and someday they will face God and give an answer for it all.

THE JUDGMENT AND THE ORGANIZATION

I had learned to fear the coming judgment. I knew I was not ready to meet God. It was no laughing matter to me. It would not be funny when I had to stand and see God face to face; not after all *I* had done! I mocked no longer. I believed instead. A soul was about to be born again into the Kingdom of God.

I realized it was useless for me to pray. My sins were too many to answer for. They were mounting steadily, and I had no Saviour to forgive me! I knew there was something between God and myself. I could not name it at the time, but I knew there was *something*.

At Romans 3:21-26 I read as follows (Berkeley Version):

But now without Law God's righteousness is revealed, as is witnessed to by the Law and the Prophets, namely, God's righteousness through faith in Jesus Christ for all believers. For there is no distinction, as all have sinned and fall short in being any glory to God. We are justified freely by

His mercy through the ransom that Christ Jesus provided; whom God put forward as a reconciling sacrifice in His blood through faith. Which was for vindication of His righteousness in forgiving the sins that previously were committed under God's forbearance, and to vindicate His righteousness in our present period, that He is just and that He accepts as just one who has faith in Jesus.

Why, that is foreign language to a Jehovah's Witness! *Should* I be able to understand it? *If* not, *why* not? Who was it written for, if not all all of us? Was I excluded?

I looked back at what had *not* been done; and it had all *not* been done in the Watch Tower organization! Quite an accomplishment: ten years of service and not a single sin forgiven! What kind of a "saviour" did I have? One who did not save? How could one what did not save be a Saviour? obviously he could not! But the Bible told me of a Saviour who saves from sin. I did not have that Saviour! But how was He to be found? The answer to that eluded me. If it was to be discovered, it would take someone other than me to find it. It did.

A FINAL RE-TAKE OF THE ORGANIZATION

Everywhere I went, I noticed that Jehovah's Witnesses were experts at getting themselves into trouble. How numerous were the cases of immorality and loose living! How many drank to excess and committed other abuses! What an environment for Christian living! I knew of several who had lost their mind and had to be committed to an institution. Was *this* God's Christian organization?

All these things I now turned over in my mind. How bound everyone was to this slave-driving organization! Oh, it all looked fine in print; but *printing* it and *living* it were two different things! That much was clearly evident!

I could now detect that there was something dangerously wrong with the idea that the Watch Tower Society was "the faithful and wise servant". Their translation of the Bible was a fraud; they knew it and refused to say or do anything about it. Their publications make statements which the Witnesses are supposed to accept merely because the Society says it. All on the authority of man-twisted Scripture! I had deserved getting fooled—putting my trust in men. I would hereafter

100

put my trust in the Lord and study His Word in its entirety, let happen what may.

February, 1957 came and I was beginning to feel strange. I no longer felt at home among Jehovah's Witnesses. Why they had never investigated the Bible like I had done I could not understand. Why should I go on any longer with a system like this?

I only attended one or two meetings that month; I learned nothing there any more. So why should I go? I could find better material in the Bible itself! Why not use the Bible alone? I knew that shortly I would depart from the organization; it would be the only honourable thing to do. I had to quit altogether.

If I did quit, I would have nothing to turn to afterward. Many thoughts entered my mind: Would I be turning my back upon God? Perhaps I was never with Him in the first place! Certainly *this* could not be His organization! Not after what I read in the Scriptures! Then where *were* His people? Did He have any? Were the churches right after all? If so, could I ever learn to accept what I once detested, hated, loathed and despised?

Then again, consider the organization! Look at those vast conventions, the world-wide "unity"! How would I feel after I left all this? Would I one day regret it and return? If so, would they accept me back? My conscience answered some of these questions for me. I knew this one elementary fact: I had been born in sin, lived in sin, and ten years in the Watch Tower organization had only added to that sin! What now? Leaving them would not remove said sin! But this one thing would be accomplished: I would be a hypocrite no longer.

Why do I say that? Because a J. W. is a first-class hypocrite; a fraud and a pretender. I was no exception. Was I really and truly a minister? *They* said I was; what did *God* think? Speaking from the Kingdom Hall platform and preaching from door-to-door was one thing; living your private life was quite another. On certain occasions servants in my home congregation got drunk; there were marital troubles and numerous other disputes. I was not exempt from my own difficulties. And yet we were all supposed to be God's people!

I was getting tired of all this hypocrisy; my own as well as everyone else's. Too many dictators in the form of servants, running other people's lives and butting into your business instead of minding their own. Constantly finding fault while maintaining that they were faultless. Seeking to have their own way in everything while denying anyone else opportunity even to be heard. Seeking favours by questionable methods. Such were our leaders!

An organization of this type just does NOT fit in with Biblical Christianity. That wasn't what Jesus Christ brought to our earth—not by a long shot! He brought something far better and finer and holier than that! He brought eternal redemption, and I was going to seek it.

By the end of February, 1957, I had seen enough. I reviewed the time I had spent within the organization. Ten years of all kinds of work—mental and physical—and for what? Now I could see the futility of it all! I saw Jehovah's Witnesses come and go! They went as they came—unsaved. What had they gained? Nothing. Same with me.

THE END NEARS

Now I could see it all clearly! No wonder they had to remove the Saviour from His position in the Godhead in the eyes of the Witnesses! The entire Watch Tower treadmill would come to a stop if the Saviour entered in! This whole idea of working for salvation was anti-Saviour (read Romans, chapter four). It was opposed to salvation full and free. We did NOT have the freedom of the sons of God! We were sold in slavery to the Watch Tower Society!

The last week in February I attended my final meeting—to resign. I was scheduled to deliver a fifteen-minute speech in the ministry school the following week, and I requested at this time that my name be taken off the roll. How I ever sat through that final meeting I will never know. How strange I felt! I knew I would never return. The Lord above would not let me!

After the meeting was over, I approached the school servant and said: "For reasons which will become manifest later, I am resigning!"

I took my final look at the Watch Tower organization from within, and knew I was stepping out into something far greater, better, and grander than I had ever imagined. I walked from the Kingdom Hall of Jehovah's Witnesses never to return. I was free!

8

The Parting Of The Ways – At Last!

REAL FREEDOM?

At least I *thought* I was free! The next evening after resigning I went to see a young friend of mine who had become a J. W. just a year previous. His parents were not Witnesses. I wanted to tell him what I had found, so I took a copy of *Jehovah of the Watchtower* over for the three of them to read. I told them I was no longer a Witness, and explained how I had resigned.

Six months later I went around to see them, I found he was no longer a Witness. But I am getting ahead of my story. As it was, it felt good to be free from the hold the organization had on me and to breathe freely once again. I did not know where I was going, if anywhere. But at least my soul was my own now.

If anyone asked me, I would have said I was an ex-Jehovah's Witness. I was glad I was out of it, and had no plans on returning. Where I would go now, or what I would do next, remained to be seen. Theologically, I had made up my mind on just one thing: The Bible taught the deity of Christ, and He was our Saviour.

I immediately wrote to some old J. W. friends of mine, friends I had during all those ten years as a J. W. I explained why I left the organization and what I believed now. I made it plain I would not return and that I was through being a Jehovah's Witness. Certainly no one would say I was a Jehovah's Witness any longer!

Barely two weeks went by, when I received a letter from the local Kingdom Hall. (See reproduction on next page.) It was unsigned, just as you see. Knowing the conniving Wit-

GERMANTOWN UNIT OF

(PHILADELPHIA COMPANY)

JEHOVAH'S WITNESSES

PHILADELPHIA 44, PA.

KINGDOM HALL

Phone: TEnnessee 9-4492

REPRESENTING
THE THEOCRACY

March 10, 1957

Mr. Ted Dencher,
3055 Martha Street,
Philadelphia 34, Pennsylvania.

Dear Ted:

Will you please be present at the meeting Friday evening,
March 15, 1957, as there are certain important questions the
Committee wants to discuss with you.

Very truly yours,

Vincent Ross

nesses as I did, I surmised what they were up to. But I was no longer one of them, and would not appear in their midst as if I were one of them. I was free and intended to remain free. However, *they* did not recognize my freedom!

I knew what they wanted. They would bring accusations against me (as a J. W.) regarding my deviation as a Witness. Why should I go, seeing I had resigned? I was no longer one of them; I had severed myself from them voluntarily. Evidently, that was not permissable! So I wrote a letter and made it official. Now they would have no excuse not to recognize my resignation! But they would not tolerate having me resign! *I* was the one who must be shown as in the wrong— the guilty party!

I did not know what had been going on "behind the scenes" until a couple weeks later. I was speaking to a J. W. friend on the telephone, and he informed me that at a recent meeting I had been disfellowshipped! Well, *that* was nice to know! It's always good to know those things and keep up with the times! How nice of them not to inform me officially! I guess they did not want to hurt my feelings!

For the benefit of the reader who may not understand how disfellowshipping is to be carried out, I quote from *Preaching Together in Unity*, a manual of discipline issued to Jehovah's Witnesses in 1955, and in use yet in 1957. Beginning on page 38 we read:

Disfellowshipping is a serious matter and means that the wrongdoer [note this word] is put out of Jehovah's New World Society. It carries with it a great responsibility and, therefore, the committee should be just and look into the matter very thoroughly.

The committee should never act on gossip, but if the charges are brought against an individual the matter must be heard by the committee.... If any members in the congregation wish to have anything to say as to whether the person should be disfellowshipped or not, they can say it at the hearing when they witness for or against the person.

Any person who is to be disfellowshipped from a congregation of Jehovah's people or is in question concerning his conduct must be notified of the time of the meeting WHEN ALL WITNESSES WILL BE PRESENT AND OF THE PURPOSE OF THE MEETING.... If he does

NOT COME TO THE MEETING ON THE DATE SET BY THE COMMITTEE, then the committee should FIND OUT WHAT DATE WOULD BE CONVENIENT TO HIM. The person SHOULD be given FULL OPPORTUNITY to make a statement and to present WITNESSES ON HIS BEHALF BEFORE THE COMMITTEE, just as the committee is willing to present their witnesses or others who are making charges. (Emphasis mine.)

There were two close J. W. friends of mine who wished to speak in my behalf—IF the committee had held a hearing, as they should have. Was I ever told WHY they wanted to see me? No! Was I given notice that I was expected to bring witnesses for my side of the story? No! Did they inform me that they would have witnesses on *their* side to press charges of wrongdoing? No! Indeed, would that meeting to which I had been invited have been a hearing at all?

In my case, it should be evident, Jehovah's Witnesses were not bound by their own rules which they set for themselves! Christianity indeed! This fact should jolt some of you Witnesses to your senses. I give this story in order to show the hypocrisy of the organization, and the two-faced method under which they operate.

Now here is the interesting part: The congregation servant called my friend from west Philadelphia AFTER I had been disfellowshipped, and asked him to write a letter, stating I had been to his home with a copy of *Thirty Years a Watchtower Slave*! My friend was more honourable than most Witnesses; he would not do it! He told the congregation servant that this would be creating evidence after sentence had been passed. But even more interesting than this: The congregation servant conferred with the circuit servant, telling him I was causing trouble, to which the circuit servant replied, "Get something on him and disfellowship him!"

All this goes to show the dirty, low, underhanded methods used by Jehovah's Witnesses when they are through with someone. It proves that:

YOU MAY NOT RESIGN FROM THE ORGANIZATION!

For full proof of this see the letter reproduced on the next page. Let us consider the letter here, in detail. Notice the

106

GERMANTOWN UNIT OF

(PHILADELPHIA COMPANY)

JEHOVAH'S WITNESSES

KINGDOM HALL
~~XXXXXXXXXXXXX~~ 419 E. Locust Ave.
Phone: TEnnessee 9-4482

PHILADELPHIA 44, PA.

REPRESENTING
THE THEOCRACY

March 31, 1957

Mr. Ted Dencher,
3055 Martha Street,
Philadelphia, Pennsylvania.

Mr. Dencher:

For some time you have taken a rebellious attitude toward the Society and the brothers, making unproven charges from the books "Jehovah of the Watchtower" and "30 Years a Prisoner of the Watchtower", going to the brother's homes with these unfounded charges, sowing discord among the brothers.

Notified by the Registered letter of March 10th 1957, of the Committee's request to appear and answer certain questions, you replied in your letter of March 13, 1957: "I am not one of Jehovah's Witnesses, I am not a part of the Watchtower organization, and hence do not come under the jurisdiction of the Watchtower Congregation Committee".

In view of the above mentioned reasons we had no alternative but to proceed with the disfellowshipping action;

Signed by the Committee.

Vincent Boss
Congregation Servant

Dominic E. Mercaldo
Assistant Congregation Servant

Fred Frobel
Bible Study Servant

See also Note on page 223.

charge: "For some time you have taken a rebellious attitude toward the Society and the brothers ..." Do you know there is no evidence to make that a fact? If you doubt this, call upon the parties involved to produce said evidence!

They continue: " ... making unproven charges from the books *Jehovah of the Watchtower* and *30 Years a Prisoner of the Watchtower*, then going to the brothers homes ..." Please, now! If you cannot get the title of the book straight, you must not have one you can produce as evidence! THERE IS NO SUCH BOOK *30 Years a Prisoner of the Watchtower*! To be fair, however, I will concede that *Thirty Years a Watchtower Slave* is alluded to. " ... with these unfounded charges ..." Were they prepared to refute every single argument in both these books? Could they go through each book paragraph by paragraph, line by line, all in one night? If so, such a meeting would have been interesting indeed! Since I feel sure that these men had never read the books at all, I would like to know of what authority they make the statement that the charges are "unfounded".

" ... sowing discord among the brothers". Do these books really do that? Then your organization must be very weak indeed! That means that if enough of these books come out and the Witnesses read them, the organization might crumble! Come on, all you converted, born-again Jehovah's Witnesses, all over the world! Put your stories in print. Herald them earth-wide! Let everyone know that the Watch Tower doctrine is heresy, and how to avoid it. Let us see how penetrating the truth can *really* be! Let us see if the darkness will not flee before the blazing light of its glory!

In the letter you will see the second reason given is that I resigned. Read it carefully. They conclude: "In view of the above mentioned reasons ..." which includes the fact that I had resigned! Resigning and taking that book over to that brother's house was what had sealed my "death warrant"!

I will admit that by resigning I had "disfellowshipped" myself from the organization as such. But *their* disfellowshipping of *me* was meant to accomplish much more. It was NOT done to get me out of the organization. It was done, rather, so that now no J. W. friend of mine could speak to me without incurring their disfavour and risking punishment. It was a venting of their wrath. To them I was now scum.

There is no honourable way out of the Watch Tower

Society. If one leaves, they will do whatever they can to blacken his name. But they only disgrace themselves by their methods. You see it takes falsehood, lies, back-biting, etc., in order to accomplish their purposes, and the lies go on and on! This fact in itself proves beyond the shadow of a doubt that it is not Christian in the slightest degree!

AFRAID OF ONE MAN WHO HAS TRUTH!

The Bible tells us at Ephesians 5:6-15 using *The New English Bible* translation:

Let no one deceive you with shallow arguments; it is for all these things that God's dreadful judgment is coming upon his rebel subjects. Have no part or lot with them. For though you were once all darkness, now as Christians you are light. Live like men who are at home in daylight, for where light is, there all goodness springs up, all justice and truth. Make sure what would have the Lord's approval; take no part in the barren deeds of darkness, but show them up for what they are. The things they do in secret it would be shameful even to mention. But everything, when once the light has shown it up, is illumined, and everything thus illumined is all light. And so the hymn says: "Awake, sleeper, rise from the dead, and Christ will shine upon you." Be most careful then how you conduct yourselves: like sensible men, not like simpletons.

Those in darkness are afraid of light. Its brilliance blinds them. They flee from it. They want it to be removed, for they cannot stand before it. So it is with Jehovah's Witnesses and *one person* who has the light! I make reference to an incident that occurred early in 1959. I was speaking in churches in Butler, Pennsylvania, and calling upon Jehovah's Witnesses in company with pastors from the area. The circuit servant was visiting the Kingdom Hall that week. That Tuesday night he announced to the congregation: "Ted Dencher is in town—*beware* of him!"

Yes—an entire congregation has to beware of one man! But again I am getting ahead of my story. I want to confine my comments as much as possible to the time when the organization and I parted company.

109

Even though I was wise to the organization by now, I still could not believe that they would sink that low! I thought there was a limit! I wrote to the Watch Tower Society and gave them the story of my disfellowshipping. I said that I intended to make matters public, nationwide, and this gave them opportunity to right any wrongs and set the matter straight. I wanted to give them the benefit of every doubt (more than they ever gave me!) A reply dated April 9, 1957 came, stating:

Now the time has come that you have severed your connections with the organization. There is no good reason why everyone in the congregation should not be advised of this fact. Consequently, you were publicly disfellowshipped and announcement was made to that effect, that you were cut off from the organization.

Take careful note of the above. Once you sever connections from the organization, you will be disfellowshipped! This implies wrongdoing. That will keep you who fear men in the organization! But it should set the rest of you free. The letter goes on to say:

As we see it, you admit the facts.... All they did was to publicly announce the fact that you were an outsider and were no longer one of Jehovah's Witnesses. They were only interested in facts and not the technicalities that were only incidental to the matter.

It was signed *Your brothers*(!), Watchtower B. & T. Society of New York, Inc.

The above is tragically comical. In order to *announce* that a person is no longer associated with them, Jehovah's Witnesses must disfellowship the individual—must treat him like a cancer! But they do, in this letter, admit that I had already voluntarily resigned! They admit that I left of my own free will! They had nothing to do with it!

Notice, in the above letter: "They [the committee] were only interested in facts and not the technicalities that were only incidental to the matter." The "technicalities" refers to the instructions in the booklet *Preaching Together in Unity*!

Did you Witnesses know that they consider such material only a list of *technicalities*? As with *The Watchtower* magazine, it is just so much ink on paper.

And so the entire organization from the top down is rank with hypocrisy—governed by the principle that "the end justifies the means". There is no good in it whatsoever. Any readers who still think so are wilfully blind.

SOME SCRIPTURAL ADMONITION

Compare these promises from the Scriptures to the promises made by the Watch Tower Society:

If, then, you have been raised with Christ, seek for things above, where Christ is seated at God's right hand. Apply your mind to things above, not to things on earth; for you have died, and your life is with Christ hidden in God. When Christ, who is our life, shall make His appearance, then we, too, shall be made to appear in glory with Him. (Colossians 3:1-4, *Berkeley*).

Do you have such a hope in your heart? You should have. What is wrong? Galatians 4:7 says: "So that thou art no longer a bondservant, but a son; and if a son, then an heir through God." Can you claim that promise as your own? Does it include you, or has someone crowded you out of the promise?

Can you understand these words of Paul: "For the law of the Spirit of life in Christ Jesus made me free from the law of sin and death" (Romans 8:2)? When did it happen to you? Romans 14:12 says: "So then each one of us shall give account of himself to God." Do you believe this? If so, you are no longer a Jehovah's Witness! Isaiah 1:18 relates: "Though your sins be as scarlet, they shall be as wool." Do you believe it? When did it happen to you?

"These things have I written unto you, that ye may KNOW that ye HAVE eternal life" (1 John 5:13). Can you claim this? Do you now HAVE eternal life, or are you yet waiting to get it? If so, John and you differ. John HAD it. John 5:24 says that the believer has passed from death unto life already. Do you accept that? Is spiritual death eternally past for you,

111

or does it appear in the future as a possibility? Either death has passed away or it has not. How is it with your soul?

A CONSIDERATION

Now look back on the entire proceedings. It would have been unfair for me to remain in the organization any longer than I did. But Jehovah's Witnesses cannot imagine anyone wanting to resign. They suspect that anyone claiming he resigned is lying. Why would one ever resign? They conclude that one must have been disfellowshipped, and for good reasons. They always want to maintain the upper hand.

These facts have been presented herein not so much to defend an individual person as to expose the false pretences of the organization. This should cause any honest Witnesses to see what their organization is really like. Their actions speak for themselves. Nothing further need be said.

Being fair about it, we should all admit that it would be unfair for a person to switch sides without disassociating from the side he is dissatisfied with. You should decide which side you want to be on and stay there. If you want to change, make a break with the side you disagree with. I attempted to do just that, only it did not work! They made it plain that there is no leaving their organization freely and voluntarily.

While I remained in the organization, I had made no attempts to work with the other side. I stuck with the organization until I felt I could no longer do so, due to my conscience. But this does not satisfy Jehovah's Witnesses. They raise other issues!

TRAITOR!

Because I speak out against them, that is what Jehovah's Witnesses have labelled me. They cannot understand why I would ever leave them and try to get others to do the same. But is not that the very thing I used to do against the churches? And I did it as a Jehovah's Witness. Now that I have changed to the other side, do you expect me to keep quiet, when I had so much to do while I was in the organization? If a person is not willing to preach what he believes, he must not believe it very strongly. Jehovah's Witnesses think it is all right for them to go and preach *their* religion, but that anyone leaving their group thereafter must be quiet!

At the very start I knew which direction to head. As I saw it, there were only two ways one could go: *away* from Christ (as I had been doing), or *to* Christ, which was what I was now doing. And so I began to recommend that way to my former associates. Why not? Should they not hear of the better way the true Christians have found?

Jehovah's Witnesses call this fighting against God—this preaching Jesus Christ as full Saviour! It makes you anti-Watch Tower. You are considered part of the "evil slave" class. It makes no difference what you turn to; if you leave them, you are an *evil slave*!

I soon found that Jehovah's Witnesses utterly reject the gospel of Jesus Christ. All literature aside from their own they label "trash". Very egotistical and bigoted, to say the least. Let my story serve as a warning before you get involved any more deeply.

FREE—BUT NOT FROM SIN'S PENALTY!

And so it was that I came free from ten years of bondage. My feelings changed considerably—for the better! Something had now been removed from between God and myself. I no longer had the feeling that a certain *something* stood between God and me.

I realized that I must now stick to the Bible, and that as a Witness I had never really been a Bible student. There was no room in their organization for a Bible student—only a *Watchtower* student. All along I had believed that they were God's organization, when in reality they had been standing *between* God and myself! Now it was different; I was free to study the Bible like I should—with an open mind.

I knew I needed a Saviour. Why? Coming free from the Watch Tower Society had not freed me from the penalty of sin. But becoming free from the penalty of sin is easier said than done!

CHRIST VERSUS THE CHRISTIANS

I have told you a little of my experience with Christians while I was in the organization. Those who *did* preach to me

8

in 1953 never expected to see me again, and I too never thought we would meet again. Now here I was, outside the organization, with nowhere to go. So I applied myself immediately to study.

I began a study of the theocratic kingdom. This study continued two years—till after my conversion (the experience which I shall soon relate). It convinced me that the Watch Tower Society was totally wrong on their "phantom kingdom" view, especially with regard to the "second coming" of Jesus Christ in 1914!

From the very outset I could see the value of individual study of the Bible free from the influences of the Society's publications. It made a difference. You could really learn something this way! And what made the biggest difference was that the Bible applied to us as *individuals* rather than as cogs on a wheel. I sensed that God placed some value on us as individuals, for Jesus died for us that way.

Christians could not easily be approached, so it seemed. They had never contacted me yet, and so I was reticent to contact them. Those who pursue strictly a pulpit ministry seldom ever reach many of the lost, except those who come to them. And do the fish usually come to the fisherman? My point here is, that I found it difficult to learn about Christ from the average Christian, whether clergyman or layman.

You may argue with Jehovah's Witnesses, but unless you really witness for Christ you argue in vain. Only the doctrine of Christ will suffice in a conversation with them. Have faith in the power of God's Word and preach *that*. Then pray that God will honour His Word that you have sown.

For the three and a half years between the time I really heard the gospel and the time I found Christ, Christians PRAYED for me. Yes, prayed—though I was purposely avoiding them. Certainly there must have been times when they felt discouraged after all that time spent in prayer, while I remained an ardent Jehovah's Witness. But they realized that *God* could act, even if they could not. So they had faith in *Him*.

Remember this one thing: To offer something to a Jehovah's Witness you have to have it yourself. If you have nothing, you may as well leave them alone. If you have a Christ-honouring testimony, give it. Back up your statements with Scriptures.

My immediate reaction was, "when in Rome do as the Romans do". I knew no other way to follow. I had no new moorings as yet. I had been disfellowshipped. I felt despondent, mainly for this reason: No other Witnesses were allowed to talk to me, and all my friends were Jehovah's Witnesses! No J. W. is allowed to speak to a disfellowshipped Witness. But they do, though—as I have found since! It shows the weakness of the Society's hold over some individuals in these matters. In some ways the Society is not as strong as they think they are!

I was cut off from all my friends, and had no one to turn to now. I would not turn to those Christians who had dealt with me in 1953, because I did not feel I was one of them (at this point). Where would I go from here? It is quite a thing, this being cut off from all acquaintances. I am glad I waited a few years before writing my story, so that the initial bitterness had time to disappear.

But at that time I was not saved; hence I abandoned myself to the "do as others do" attitude. I found out that kind of thing does not satisfy, either. Short-lived pleasure cures no ills. It left nothing profitable within. So I decided to throw myself on the mercy of God, come what may. I was not dominated by a master-mind organization anymore. Now I had no one but God to answer to; it was better this way.

One time a Witness friend asked me where I found this new-found faith. When I held up a copy of the Bible that I used in the door-to-door work, she refused to believe it, and merely scoffed. To her it was unbelievable that anything other than Watch Tower propaganda could be found in the Bible. The J. W.'s will not accept the real answer, so they resort to speculation. They assume some church or denomination talked me into becoming what I am now.

Some Witnesses think I have "gone to the dogs"! Wishful thinking! Others wonder what happened between the organization and me to cause the "rift". Now you have the answer officially, right from the Society! How do you feel now?

SALVATION NEARS

I made no plans to attend any church or join any group. I knew of none to join up with. What I was waiting for I do not know. I knew I was not pretending any longer. I knew of no way of approaching God. If He and I were to come to terms, He would have to approach me! It was spring of 1957, and I was getting over the shock of leaving Jehovah's Witnesses and settling down to a normal way of living. Then it happened—*He* came to *me*!

One night in Philadelphia I was walking along a street and I stopped. I had been meditating upon the Saviour. Yes, I mused, surely His blood shed at Calvary was what mattered for salvation! That was all that was basically essential for our salvation. He came to earth to die for us; and He fulfilled that purpose at Calvary. Surely this was God's plan, that we believe upon Him and accept Him as our Saviour!

Why I had stopped I do not know. My attention was caught up to the sky. My mind went back two thousand years—back to Calvary. In my mind's eye, so clearly I could almost see it as it flashed across my mind, was the cross. And God the Saviour hung upon it, dying for me.

I was terrified—awestruck. The sight horrified me. It had never seemed so real to me before. No wonder they walked away from that cross; I might have fled. Then, in a manner that I am at a loss for words to explain, I realized the real truth: HE HAD DIED FOR ME! As I gazed upward, I repeated these words, twice: "He died for me! He died for *me*!"

O Christian! You never told me this! He won me at Calvary. His love poured out there *wooed* me like nothing I had ever experienced before. To think that I waited ten years for this! It was worth it all!

WHAT NEXT?

I began to pray—as a Christian. From that night in which I beheld Christ, I believed. Yes, I had received faith! And in faith I had received Him as my Saviour. And so it was that I came to know God through Jesus Christ. But I was not expecting what was to follow. A short while later a strange thing happened.

THE FINAL QUESTION

I received a letter in the mail from one of those Christians

116

who had dealt with me back in 1953. Just a letter concerning some church activities. But it came like a bolt from the blue. I responded by writing and giving the entire story of what had been happening to me. I began the letter by saying, "It's strange, your writing to me just now; I have broken off relations with the Watch Tower Society." Then followed the story of what had happened. I received a reply, and in it was a strange question. I was now twenty-six years old, but had never yet been asked this question. I was asked: "Ted, what do you think of Jesus Christ?"

I had to make a decision in my heart, and confess that decision. I was not ashamed to declare what I now thought of the risen Lord. And so I made what I now consider to be a conservative statement, replying: "I have come to accept Christ as God, and as my personal Saviour." That was all. I am glad he did not question me about the many other doctrines of the Christian faith! But on this subject I was ready to declare myself without reservation.

THE FINALITY

I knew from my studies that He came to offer substitutionary atonement for me. He sought me till He found me; then He put His arms around me, and brought me home!

I knew not what would happen now. I had made my decision; now I must wait—upon God. Christian—you know what happened next! As it happened to you, so it happened to me.

But read on—I will explain *how* it happened.

9

Salvation Comes – O Glorious Day!

REDEEMED!

I had been born again, but at the moment did not know it. Just as soon as I signed my name and sent that letter off, things began to happen. I did not *ask* for them to happen. All I knew was, I felt that peace which passes understanding; I felt at ease with God. Gone was the feeling of loneliness that had come from being cast off from my friends. Gone too, were my sins—lost in the sea of God's forgetfulness!

As these new feelings began to flood my soul, I began to feel a change in my attitude towards others; I could enjoy the fellowship of Christians. The letter I had sent soon became a public confession, as it made the rounds of those interested. Before long, I was invited over for a time of fellowship; there they brought to my attention the first scripture I was to learn as a Christian—Romans 8:2.

I could understand it! Why? Because I had experienced what the writer of that verse had experienced! That is why he wrote it! I knew I was free from the law of sin and death! But could it really be true? I had been tricked and fooled for over ten years; this time I must step carefully, I mused, to be sure I'll not be fooled again. IF this is of God, He will continue what He has begun! And so I began to seek out His presence and will in prayer and by reading the Bible. I found Him ever near to hear my petition.

I felt the presence of the Holy Spirit, whose personal existence I had denied all those ten years. Oh, how He could lead and comfort! But now that I had begun to seek out the Christian way, I wanted to be careful to do *His* will, and not my own. I wanted to find my place in the church and be baptized, but yet I must await His directing hand.

118

There would be no hurry now. My frantic pace of buying and selling was over; now I was safe in His love and care—forever! "I will *never* leave thee nor forsake thee!" "Lo, I am with you *always*, even to the end of the world!" What assuring promises! *He* would take care of me and use me *as* He wished, *when* He wished.

And so I waited six months before I entered the church. The family who had so kindly dealt with me in 1953 became my spiritual parents and I benefited greatly from their counsel and advice. Sad to say that this family is now on the verge of divorce (see 2 Peter 1:10). I attended services at the church where I faced those who had cast me out when I was a Witness. But as for church membership, I was waiting for God to choose the church of *His* choice for me.

During those six months I studied the Bible. I prayed more and more. I felt that sweet, mystic union of His spirit with mine, bearing witness that I was now a child of God. Oh what I had missed for all these years! The joy of sins forgiven is one that simply cannot be put into suitable speech. It defies description. It must be experienced to be realized. All I can say is that Romans 8:1 now made sense to me: "There is therefore now no condemnation to them that are in Christ Jesus."

BLESSED ASSURANCE

Dear reader, do you know what it means to be in Christ Jesus? Do you know what it means for *you* to be *His*, and for *Him* to be *yours*? If *you* are not *His*, then *He* is not *yours*! I can understand this now. John 5:24 became precious to me: "Verily, verily, I say unto you, He that heareth my word, and believeth him that sent me, HATH ETERNAL LIFE, and COMETH NOT INTO JUDGMENT, BUT HATH PASSED OUT OF DEATH INTO LIFE."

Never before in my life had the Bible moved me to tears. The love of God became almost too great for me to bear; there were times when I had to request God to HOLD BACK His presence in times of prayer and meditation, for I could only stand so much in my mortal body. I have literally felt the living presence of the Holy Spirit. On two occasions I received visible manifestations, when I was yet very young

119

in the Lord and seeking assurance from Him in prayer. I have tangibly felt the presence of the Lord at my side on several occasions.

But to pray, and to know that my prayer was being heard, and then to have it answered, was truly beyond my comprehension. Why should He so hear my plea? Who can understand it? Why should the holy God stoop to commune with such as I? I will never know, perhaps, until I see Him face to face. Then I shall know as I am known.

My dear reader, do you know what it is to pray and KNOW that your prayer is being heard? Do you rest serenely in the knowledge that at the moment you die you go to be with Him? Do you know that He is ever with you, to walk through death's dark valley with you, and guide you safely through? Do you? I do.

Is it well with your soul? Has your old account of sin been settled? He gives perfect peace and assurance to those who seek and ask for it of Him.

HIS EVER-PRESENT POWER

Dear friend, did you ever have this happen to you? One night, while upon my pillow, the burdens of life lay heavily upon me. I was weighed down, stumbling under their heavy weight. I was oppressed, sick at heart and very worried. I knew I could not sleep that night. There were so many things going wrong—and I could see no way out. I recalled a verse of Scripture—1 Peter 5:7: "Casting all your care upon Him, for he careth for you." With full trust in His promise, I prayed "Oh Lord, I cast my cares fully upon *thee*!" Yes, with all the boldness that it took to speak in such a vein to God, I cast my cares upon Him. And He took them. And He soothed my troubled mind. And I felt the burdens roll away, like a heavy load from off my shoulder. And I went to sleep.

My friend, have you ever had Satan come into your life in a moment's time, and interfere so powerfully that you could not even pray? Or have you ever had him cut off your prayer? I have had it happen. I knew the evil source of this power. I was helpless to combat it. I could do nothing. In my utter helplessness I could not even call upon God for help. In hopeless despair I knew not what to do. I was at the mercy of the

Evil One. A chilling coldness crept over my soul. I was in this power; would I fall under his control?

The Bible tells us: "Great peace have they that love thy law; And they have no occasion of stumbling" (Psalms 119: 165). "Oh that thou wouldest hearken to my commandments! then had thy peace been as a river, and thy righteousness as the waves of the sea" (Isaiah 48:13). At that moment when He seemed farthest away, He was near. His peace flooded my soul and in one moment's time the power of the enemy was *broken*! Such experiences are the lot of all those redeemed.

To tell you of all that I have received at the hand of the Lord would fill this entire chapter and more. He is my constant Friend and Guide, and has never failed me, though I have failed Him countless times. How can I ignore such love as He gives?

Finally, after six months of walking close to Him, He led me into the fellowship of the church, where I was baptized in the triune name and received communion. In just a few months I began to receive invitations to speak at prayer meetings, etc., to give my testimony. I spoke at various religious gatherings. Then I received my first pulpit assignment. Since then I have received many invitations to speak in churches. I praise the Lord for the opportunity to do so.

CHRISTIAN HELP

I received much wonderful spiritual help from the Christians who originally spoke to me about Christ. This sort of thing is very necessary when you are just beginning to grow in the Lord. There should be an increase of grace-growth in the life of *every* Christian, and without exception. To this end I needed guidance and counsel from those who had walked in this path. I appreciated it deeply.

I also received the loving encouragement I needed. Discouragement came, as it always does, whether you ask for it or not; but I stayed close to the Lord's side and always came through. Events happened quite rapidly, of course, as they still do in my life. I was not saved to a life of ease and do-nothingness! I was saved to work in the Master's vineyard until He comes. I intend to remain busy at it while He spares my life for such purpose.

Eventually the time came when I had to face my former brethren; those with whom I had worked for many years as a Jehovah's Witness. Could I stand this test? A friend and I went to Yankee Stadium, to a J. W. convention, to hand out gospel tracts. We went to hear part of that day's sessions. The hold they had on me was gone! It was the greatest test I had had to confront thus far—facing the Witnesses with the gospel of Christ. But the Lord had called me for this purpose, among others.

It would have been the easiest thing in the world for me to retreat within the safety of some church and "hide" there! But God bade me go right into the midst of Jehovah's Witnesses (as I've done at many of their conventions, and still do!) and make the gospel known among them. The Holy Spirit has been our portion during these occasions, and our hearts have been filled with singing, even while surrounded by those who hate us and the gospel we bear.

Yes, they hate the gospel. I have seen many Witnesses take a gospel tract containing Scriptures and tear it to shreds. That, my dear friends, is what they think of the precious Saviour who died for them.

Yet I have seen ardent Witnesses melt before the Word of God. I have seen servants and pioneers overcome with the truth of the sacred text. Yes, it is reaching them by the tens of thousands. I hope no one will ever refuse to speak to a Jehovah's Witness about the Lord and what He can do for them.

DOCTRINES

Jehovah's Witnesses think that Christians have to agree on every single doctrine in the Bible. It has never been that way, and is not so presently. One does not have to have all these doctrines straight in his mind in order to be saved. One is saved through faith in the Lord Jesus Christ, and by means of Him only. Therefore it is essential to learn about *Him* in order to be saved. The other teachings of the Bible will become clear eventually, when, with the aid of the Holy Spirit, the new-born Christian begins to read and study the Word.

As I began searching the Scriptures these various doctrines began to get clearer all the time. For example, I could see clearly that the doctrine of the *soul*, as taught in the Bible, differed from what the Watch Tower Society teaches about it. (For full details of this doctrine, please see chapter twelve.) The more I read the Bible, the clearer it all became. I did not hurry, but took my time.

It is the same with the doctrine of eternal punishment, which involves a future judgment. Hebrews 9:27, 28 reads: "And inasmuch as it is appointed unto men once to die, and after this cometh judgment; so Christ also, having been once offered to bear the sins of many, shall appear a second time, apart from, to them that wait for him, unto salvation" (*A.S.V.*). Jehovah's Witnesses do not accept any of this. They rejected it all long ago.

FURTHER STUDY

As I began to speak in churches, I was asked all kinds of questions by Christians of many denominations. This sharpened my own knowledge and caused me to study even further. The amazing thing is, once your faith in the *organization* has been weakened, your faith and trust in the *Bible* are strengthened! As you lose confidence in *men*, you gain confidence in *God*. The more you distrust the Watch Tower Society, the more you trust the *Bible*!

But Jehovah's Witnesses cannot understand the structure of the church. They cannot understand how it can be of God and yet have various denominations that differ with each other in points of theology. With their critical attitude they never will understand.

Christians who have a wishy-washy faith, a "maybe there is or maybe there isn't" attitude about religion, usually are not worth much to the church. But I am not advocating a final dogmatism beyond which there is no further perusal. On certain details of doctrine I believe we will have to await the hereafter for the final answer. In the meantime we should all endeavour to get our faith straight in our own mind in order to give a good, sensible, coherent explanation of it. We of the conservative or evangelical faith do not say *we* are 100 per cent right and all our fellow worshippers with differing views are wrong; neither do we compromise our own beliefs for expediency. We hold our own convictions and teach them. Yet we respect the other man's opinion and his right to it.

However, before a person has become a Christian doctrinal accuracy is not the primary issue; the basic question is: what have you done with Christ?—is He your Saviour?

Each one knows in his own heart whether or not he has been born from above. Whether or not you will admit this one way or the other, you still know. There is a difference between a person who is *trying* to be a Christian and a person who *is* a Christian. I am not trying to bring Jehovah's Witnesses into the organized Church. They must first come to Christ, *then* they may take their place in the Church. Until they themselves have been changed they can only be welcomed as unbelievers.

After you have come to Christ and found your place in the Church, all the various problems that the various denominations seem to create will begin to clear up for you. All things having become new, the Church will now appear in a different light. No longer will Satan blind you, but, as a son of God, you will be able to see things that are spiritual and comprehend them.

Never let the hypocrisy of others stumble you, or use it as an excuse. Remember, that it is *Christ's* church, and He is its Master. Regardless of the external state of the church, your eternal destiny is at stake. Do not permit anything to stand in your way on the road to eternal life in Jesus Christ. When I was searching the Scriptures I left the church out of the picture altogether. If you are looking for a church with which you will totally agree before you find Christ, you will pass on into eternity with your search unrewarded.

I have gone into this because of the stumbling-block the church seems to be for Jehovah's Witnesses. I have found no objection to the system of the clergy and their titles as found within the church. Do not read things into the Scriptures that are not there. Pray earnestly that God will enlighten you further in this matter. But now I wish to leave this subject, and show the reader what I began to learn as regards the historic, orthodox faith, still preached faithfully today.

THE DEITY OF CHRIST UNFOLDS

I will deal rather briefly with this subject here, as chapter eleven explains this in full detail. There is nothing like the new birth to convince a person who and what Jesus Christ is. The majority of those denying the deity of Jesus Christ are usually found to be among the unsaved.

Having been changed from an enemy of Christ into His friend, I was now more than ever desirous of learning all I could about Him. I wanted to delve into the Word and see what it would reveal about Him. This I did.

I was amazed at how all through the Bible you find the mystery of the unity between the Father, Son and Holy Spirit. From the very beginning one reads: "And God said, Let US make man in OUR image, after OUR likeness.... And God created man in HIS own image, in the image of God created HE him; male and female created HE them" (Genesis 1:26, 27). This again occurs at Genesis 11:7, 8 when the tongues were confused at the tower of Babel: "Come, let US go down, and there confound their language.... So JEHOVAH scattered them abroad from thence upon the face of all the earth" (*A.S.V.*).

The Jews of Jesus' day recognized the fact that He claimed to be more than just a man. The dispute was over His deity (the same dispute Jehovah's Witnesses have today!) At John 5:18 we read: "For this reason the Jews continued to seek the more eagerly to put him to death, because not only was he breaking the Sabbath, but he was actually speaking of God as his own Father, thus making himself God's equal" (*The New Testament in Modern English*, Montgomery).

Although the Watch Tower Bible at John 1:1 reads "The Word was a god", we read further at Deuteronomy 32:39: "See now that I, even I, am he, and there is NO GOD WITH ME." *The Septuagint Version of the Greek Old Testament and Apocrypha*, English translation by Sir Launcelot Lee Brenton, published by Samuel Bagster and Sons Limited, London, reads as follows: IDETE IDETE HOTI EGO EIMI KAI OUK ESTI THEOS PLEN EMOU—"Behold, behold that I am *he*, and there is no god beside me." The expression *ego eimi* occurs here, and at John 8:58 He becomes to Jesus Christ! If the Watch Tower idea of God were true, then the Bible would be contradicting *itself* and the Holy Spirit contradicting *Himself*. This fact alone proves the Watch Tower translation of John 1:1 to be a fraud.

JESUS AS THE MESSIAH

Did Jesus become the Messiah (or *Christ*) at the age of

thirty as the doctrine of adoptionism (taught by Jehovah's Witnesses) claims? The Bible says: "For there is born to you this day in the city of David a Saviour, WHO IS CHRIST [*Messiah*] the Lord" (Luke 2:11). Either He was or He was not. The Bible says He was! Again we read: "For to what angel did God ever say, 'You are my Son, today I have become your Father'? Or again, 'I will become His Father, and He shall become my Son'? But when He brings again His first-born into the world, He says, 'And let all the angels worship Him'." (Hebrews 1:5, 6 *The New Testament,* Williams).

If Jesus was not born the Christ, then the Christ child was not born. That is why Jehovah's Witnesses hold no reverence whatsoever for the Christmas season or celebration. They deny that the Christ child was born; teaching instead, that this Jesus later *became* the Christ or Messiah.

As for His death, they teach the false doctrine that Jesus was annihilated. When resurrection morning came there was no one inside the tomb to be raised, they say. They have taught from the beginning that the body of Jesus never rose from the tomb. They think His body disappeared completely sometime after its burial. Since nobody was in the tomb (after the alleged annihilation) then *that* is exactly who was raised—*nobody*! How could someone who does not exist be resurrected? Created again, perhaps yes; but resurrected, no! That is why Jehovah's Witnesses hold no reverence or respect for the Easter season. They deny the resurrection of Jesus Christ and teach instead that He was re-created—as an invisible spirit. Paul said: "If Christ has not been raised, then our preaching counts for nothing and your faith is groundless" (1 Corinthians 15:14, *The Simplified New Testament,* Norlie).

WATCHTOWER SALVATION

According to the Watch Tower Society, salvation is nothing more than being given a second chance to start all over from where Adam and Eve began! It is another chance for the human race to right itself. They advocate that we have been relieved of Adamic or hereditary sin, and nothing more. They believe that Jesus was a "second Adam" and nothing more. He came to give His *life,* not to die but to *live* for us! The shed blood of Christ and the subsequent resurrection mean next to nothing to the Witnesses. Quoting from *Studies in the Scriptures,* Volume V (By Charles Taze Russell) we read on page 443:

So far as Justice was concerned, the Jews might have put our Lord to death in any form, and the requirements of Justice have been equally well met. The necessary thing was surrender of his innocent soul (being) as an off-set or in exchange for a guilty soul (being) whose existence was forfeited through transgression. Neither was it necessary, so far as the ransom feature was concerned, that our Lord's person should be wounded, and his blood literally shed or spilled on the ground.

The Witnesses believe that the perfect life lived by Jesus gives us the opportunity to *earn* our salvation. They believe this is accomplished by selling Watch Tower books, magazines and pamphlets, attending Kingdom Hall regularly and going to the conventions. Every Jehovah's Witness dies without the assurance of salvation. All this because he trusted men and rejected the Lord Jesus Christ as his personal Saviour.

We have a much better Saviour than the one described by the Watch Tower Society. *Salvation* brought about the change in my life, and that salvation came through God the Son, who is my personal Saviour. I am glad my salvation came the way it did. No one can point their finger and say so-and-so converted me! In the final analysis we can say that my salvation came by means of no man. True, men pointed the way; but the transformation came from God alone.

After I had accepted Jesus Christ as my own personal Saviour, then the change came. Not before. Then the assurance entered my heart, never to be taken away! It is the work of the Holy Spirit to keep strengthened within me the faith that began with Christ. Because of Him I cannot fall.

WILL IT COME TO OTHERS?

Whether or not it comes to others depends upon their reaction to Jesus Christ. I cannot recommend that you follow the way I came, for others may come differently. You would do well to place yourself under the influence of the gospel by attending a church that preaches and teaches the gospel.

You might also begin a Bible study; many courses are currently available to you. In the end, however, it will be whether or not you have received Jesus Christ as your Saviour that determines your eternal destiny.

Do not come because I came. Come because YOU YOURSELF WANT TO COME. Let no man draw or hinder you. Make it a matter between the Lord and yourself. Be assured of this: You will never find Christ so long as you remain an active Jehovah's Witness.

10

Is Dis-association Necessary For Salvation?

Some may wonder why it is necessary to dis-associate from Jehovah's Witnesses to be saved, or even question the advisability of it. This raises a technical question: Can a Jehovah's Witness be saved? We will investigate this subject and answer it in a little while.

To begin with, the organization will not tolerate any views but their own. Their viewpoint of the new birth is expressed in *Make Sure of All Things* in these words:

> "Born again" means a birthlike realization of prospects and hopes for spirit life by resurrection to heaven. Such a realization is brought about through the water of God's truth in the Bible and God's holy spirit, his active force.

They believe that these "born again" ones are numbered at 144,000:

> (Gr., *ek.kle.si'a*—"assembly", "congregation") An assembly of persons called out from this world to the services of Almighty God. The Christian congregation, the "holy nation", is comprised of Jesus Christ, the Head, and 144,000 members of his body. The term also applies collectively to all those of the anointed spiritual class on earth at any particular time, or to the local assembly in any place. (*Ek.kle.si'a* is often translated "church".)

In order to attain to the new birth, they teach one must be saved (i.e., made a recipient of salvation). What is the official Watch Tower teaching on the subject of salvation? Again we look at the book.*Make Sure of All Things*:

9

Salvation is the deliverance from the destructive power of sin, a redemption from the ultimate end of sin which is everlasting death, annihilation. It means a restoration to divine favour and perfection after having sinned or missed God's mark of perfection set for faithful mankind. Salvation as referred to in the Bible may either be (1) the preserving of one alive from trouble or an impending disaster or (2) the opportunity to receive everlasting life in a state of peace, happiness and prosperity. Salvation is not an act of divine justice but rather an act of divine mercy. It is a justification or a being declared righteous granted by God the Superior to a handicapped inferior. As an act of mercy it is the withholding (1) of the consequences of disaster or (2) of the punishment of everlasting death (annihilation) when either is justly due for failure to keep the divine law. Salvation that counts is not a self-salvation, a salvation by works, a salvation by law or a universal salvation, as these are all unclean religious fallacies.

So according to the Watch Tower Society, to be "born again" (which they pervert to suit their heresy) you have to be one of the 144,000! Since they teach the number was sealed in 1931, you can have no hope of being born again—if you were baptized from 1932 onward!

Speaking of the non-144,000, the supposed "earthly class", the book *New Heavens And a New Earth* states on page 209:

As the facts show, they do not have a baptism and anointing of God's spirit along with a baptism into Christ's body and into his kind of death, a death that parts with all prospect of perfect human life in the new world. Nonetheless, they do enjoy a special baptism besides their immersion in water. That baptism today is into the Greater Noah.

As a present-day Jehovah's Witness, therefore, you have given up all hope of ever being born again, and thus becoming a child of God. You have relinquished your right to become born again and become a recipient of the Holy Spirit. By your stand you claim that the adoption of the sons of God does not apply to you. You refused to become crucified with Christ and risen with Him in the new nature. You refuse to become Spirit-begotten. You lay no claim upon salvation. By your rejection of salvation you indicate that you consider Christ's sacrifice for you unnecessary (except to provide for you the opportunity to gain eternal life on earth)—and without effect upon your life, both present and future. Thereby, in every sense of the word, you have wholeheartedly rejected the Lord and Saviour, Jesus Christ!

CAN A CHRIST-REJECTOR BE BORN AGAIN?

Actually, this is a technicality. How so? Well, at the moment you accept Christ as your Saviour you are no longer rejecting Him. You turn from this rejection and receive Him into your heart. From the moment that you turn away from your rejection of Him, from that moment on you are no longer a Jehovah's Witness. You have left the organization and their vain imaginations behind!

So far in this chapter we have given only the Watch Tower side of the story of conversion and the new birth. What does the Bible say? Keep in mind that this is discussed in detail later on in this book. However, here we want to consider a number of Scriptures concerning these subjects.

BECOME CONVERTED

"Then will I teach transgressors thy ways; and sinners shall be converted to thee," says Psalm 51:13. "Know ye, that he who converteth a sinner from the error of his way shall save a soul from death, and shall cover a multitude of sins" (James 5:20). "Zion shall be redeemed with justice, and her converts with righteousness" (Isaiah 1.27). "Verily I say unto you, Except ye be converted, and become as little children, ye shall not enter the kingdom of heaven" (Matthew 18:3). "Repent ye therefore, and be converted, that your sins may be blotted out" (Acts 3:19). "The doctrine of the Lord is perfect, converting the soul" (Psalm 19:7).

Yes, the Bible definitely teaches that a person must be *converted*!

REPENTANCE NECESSARY

"Repent ye therefore, and turn again, that your sins may

be blotted out, that so there may come seasons of refreshing from the presence of the Lord" (Acts 3:19). "The times of ignorance therefore God overlooked; but now he declareth to men that they should be everywhere repent" (Acts 17:30).

You must repent of your sins (change your attitude of mind and heart concerning them) in order to be saved.

CONFESSION OF CHRIST

"Therefore, everyone who confesses Me before men I will also acknowledge before My Father in heaven" (Matthew 10: 32, *The Simplified New Testament*). "Keep contending in the noble contest of the faith; seize hold on eternal life, to which you were called when you confessed the good confession in the presence of many witnesses" (1 Timothy 6:12, *The New Testament in Modern English*). Or, as Weymouth's translation reads: "Struggle your hardest in the good contest for the faith; seize hold of eternal life, to which you were called; you made the good confession before many witnesses."

"Anyone who confesses (acknowledges, owns) that Jesus is the Son of God, God abides (lives, makes His home) in him, and he (abides, lives, makes his home) in God" (1 John 4:15, *Amplified New Testament*). "This letter is to assure you that you have eternal life. It is addressed to those who give their allegiance to the Son of God" (1 John 5:13, *The New English Bible*). Do you feel assured that you presently possess eternal life? Anyone who believes in Him shall have eternal life and *know* it!

RECOGNITION OF THE NEW BIRTH

If you have been born from above you will certainly know it and declare it unashamedly. You will be drawn to God and the Christian Church. You will love the brethren worldwide. You will cause no divisions within the Church. You will pray for the success of the Church and the proclamation of the gospel. You will do as directed by the Holy Spirit. God will become your teacher. "So much for those who would mislead you. But as for you, the anointing which you received from him stays with you; you need no other teacher, but learn all you need to know from his initiation, which is real and no illusion" (1 John 2:26, 27 *The New English Bible*).

132

After you have come to Christ you will still face the same problems you always faced, and will suffer many trials. You may be tested sorely at times. But He will bring you through your every experience victoriously.

There may be times when you will feel as if you were out of fellowship with the Lord. Let nothing discourage you or hinder your spiritual progress. Wait upon the Lord and pray. Yours will be the victory. Do not compare yourself with others. Remember this one thing: You have been born again because of His *mercy* toward you!

Ever be mindful of the precious promise of God: "Being confident of this very thing, that he who began a good work in you will perfect it until the day of Jesus Christ" (Philippians 1:6).

IS THE NEW BIRTH THE ONLY WAY TO SALVATION?

"Except a man be born again, he cannot see the kingdom of God" (John 3:3). Moffatt's translation (1901) reads: "Unless a man be born from above, he cannot see the reign of God." Jesus said this is accomplished as follows: "Except a man be born of water and the Spirit, he cannot enter into the kingdom of God" (John 3:5). What is the difference between your physical birth and your new birth? "That which is born of the flesh is flesh; and that which is born of the Spirit is spirit" (John 3:6). This defies explanation: "The Spirit breathes where it will, and thou hearest its voice, but thou knowest not when it comes, or where it goes; thus it is with every one who has been born of the Spirit" (John 3:8, *The Emphatic Diaglott*).

This subject of the new birth is discussed by John Wesley, as found in *The Works of John Wesley*, Volume VI, page 65:

If any doctrines within the whole compass of Christianity may be properly termed fundamental, they are doubtless these two,—the doctrine of justification, and that of the new birth: the former relating to that great work which God does *for us*, in forgiving our sins; the latter, to the great work which God does *in us*, in renewing our fallen nature.

Reading now from the above-named volume, page 69:

Before a child is born into the world he has eyes, but sees not; he has ears, but does not hear. He has a very imperfect use of any other sense. He has no knowledge of any of the things of the world, or any natural understanding. . . .

While a man is in a mere natural state, before he is born of God, he has, in a spiritual sense, eyes and sees not; a thick, impenetrable veil lies upon them; he has ears, but hears not; he is utterly deaf to what he is most of all concerned to hear. His other spiritual senses are all locked up: He is in the same condition as if he had them not. . . . But as soon as he is born of God, there is a total change in all these particulars.

His ears being opened, he is now capable of hearing the inward voice of God, saying, "Be of good cheer; thy sins are forgiven thee;" "go and sin no more."

From thence it manifestly appears what is the nature of the new birth. It is that great change which God works in the soul when he brings it into new life; when he raises it from the death of sin to the life of righteousness. It is the change wrought in the whole soul by the Almighty Spirit of God when it is "created anew in Christ Jesus"; when it is "renewed after the image of God, in righteousness and true holiness"; when the love of the world is changed into the love of God. . . .

It is not difficult for any who has considered these things, to see the necessity of the new birth, and to answer the Third question, Wherefore, to what end, is it necessary that we should be born again? . . . Men may indeed flatter themselves (so desparately wicked and so deceitful is the heart of man!) that they [because of their own morality] may live with God; and thousands do really believe, that they have found a broad way which leadeth not to destruction.

Wesley's concluding remarks on this subject can be found on page 77:

Let this therefore, if you have not already experienced this inward work of God, be your continual prayer: "Lord, add this to all thy blessings,—let me be born again! Deny whatever thou pleasest, but deny not this; let me be 'born from above!' Take away whatsoever seemeth thee good,—reputation, fortune, friends, health,—only give me this, to be born of the Spirit, to be received among the children of God! Let me be born, 'not of corruptible seed, but incorruptible, by the word of God, which liveth and abideth for ever'; and then let me daily 'grow in grace, and in the knowledge of our Lord and Saviour Jesus Christ!' "

THE BLOOD OF CHRIST SUFFICES FOR SALVATION

Not by blood and works, but through the blood alone. "The blood of Jesus Christ cleanses us from all sin" (1 John 1:7). In Revelation the overcomers of Satan "overcame him BECAUSE OF THE BLOOD OF THE LAMB, and because of the word of their testimony" (Revelation 12:11).

The entire body of Spirit-born ones, the Church, was "purchased with his own blood" (Acts 20:28). Justification is through the blood alone: "Much more then, being now JUSTIFIED BY HIS BLOOD, shall we be SAVED FROM THE WRATH OF GOD through him" (Romans 5:9).

Forgiveness and redemption—all through the blood: "In whom we have our REDEMPTION THROUGH HIS BLOOD, the forgiveness of our trespasses, according to the riches of his grace" (Ephesians 1:7). Sanctification comes through the blood: "Wherefore Jesus also, that he might SANCTIFY THE PEOPLE THROUGH HIS OWN BLOOD, suffered without the gate" (Hebrews 13:12).

Let us consider the words of John 6:47-58, using Moffatt's 1935 translation:

"Truly, truly I tell you, the believer has eternal life. I am the bread of life. Your ancestors ate manna in the desert, but they died; the bread that comes down from heaven is such that one eats of it and never dies. I am the living bread which has come down from heaven; if anyone eats of this bread, he will live forever; and more, the bread that I give is my flesh, given for the life of the world."

The Jews then wrangled with one another, saying, "How can he give us His flesh to eat?" So Jesus said to them, "Truly, truly I tell you, unless you eat the flesh of the Son of man and drink his blood, you have no life within you.

He who feeds on my flesh and drinks my blood possesses
eternal life (and I will raise him up on the last day), for
my flesh is real food and my blood is real drink.

"He who feeds on my flesh and drinks my blood remains
within me, as I remain within him. Even as the living
Father sent me and I live by the Father, so he who feeds
on me will also live by me. Such is the bread which has
come down from heaven: your ancestors ate their bread
and died, but he who feeds on this bread will live forever."

By faith we drink his blood, and live!

FAITH—NOT FEELINGS!

The miracle of the new birth is realized by faith—not mere
feelings. Any emotional experiences you had are immaterial
to your actual salvation, if you possess it. Barnabas is re-
ported as being " a good man, and full of the Holy Spirit
and of FAITH" (Acts 11:24). So it must be with you.

A wonderful and outstanding account of faith versus works
(hence, faith versus outside influences) is given by Paul in the
fourth chapter of Romans. Quoting verses 1 through 16, according to the Weymouth translation:

What shall we say of Abraham, our natural forefather?
For if he was held to be righteous on the ground of his
actions, he has something to boast of. Yes, but not in the
presence of God. For what says the Scripture? 'ABRA-
HAM BELIEVED GOD, AND THIS WAS CREDITED
TO HIM AS RIGHTEOUSNESS" (Gen. 15:6). But in
the case of a man who works, pay is not reckoned as a
favour but as something due; whereas in the case of a man
who in place of working believes in Him who acquits the
ungodly, his faith is credited to him as righteousness.
In this way David also tells of the blessedness of the
man whom God credits with righteousness apart from his
actions.... For ABRAHAM'S FAITH—so we affirm—
WAS CREDITED TO HIM AS RIGHTEOUSNESS
(Gen. 15:6). In what circumstances, then? Was it after he
had been circumcised, or before? Before, not after.
Again, the promise that he should inherit the world did
not come to Abraham or his posterity through law, but

through righteousness depending on faith. For if it is to those who rely on Law who are heirs, then faith is useless and the promise counts for nothing.

All depends on faith for this reason—that righteousness may be by grace, so that the promise should be made sure to all his posterity; not merely to those who rely on the Law, but also to those who rely on faith like Abraham's. For in the sight of God in whom he believed, who gives life to the dead and speaks on things non-existent as though existing, Abraham is the father of all of us.

Tying in the death and resurrection of Christ with the above, Paul continues on; quoting from verse 24 of the fourth chapter to chapter five, verse 5:

Faith is going to be credited to us who believe in Him who raised Jesus, our Lord, from the dead, who was delivered up because of our offences, and was raised to life for our acquittal. Acquitted then as a result of faith, let us enjoy peace with God through our Lord Jesus Christ, through whom we have been brought by our faith into the position of favour in which we stand, and we exult in hope of seeing God's glory.

And not only so: we also exult in our afflictions, knowing as we do that affliction produces endurance; endurance, ripeness of character; and ripeness of character, hope; and that this hope never disappoints, because God's love for us floods our hearts through the Holy Spirit, who has been given to us.

FAITH WITHOUT WORKS?

Yes, at least the type of works such as performed by Jehovah's Witnesses! Let us consider one of the favourite texts of the Witnesses, James 2:17—but let us read it within the context. We here use Weymouth's translation:

What good is it, my brethren, if a man professes to have faith, and yet his actions do not correspond? Can such faith save him? Suppose a brother and a sister are poorly clad or lack daily food, and one of you says to them, "Fare you well; keep yourselves warm and well fed," and yet you do not supply their bodily needs; what is the use of that? So also faith, if it is unaccompanied by obedience, is dead in itself.

Jehovah's Witnesses care little for the social welfare of others (except their own kind, like the Pharisees of old). They let others shift for themselves, while they go about selling literature. The following from the appendix to the Weymouth translation, regarding James 2:23, is appropriate here (from page 693):

It is rather curious at first sight to find the Epistle of James quoting this text [Genesis 15:6] in a demonstration that justification requires deeds as well as faith. There is no real contradiction. What James is rebuking is faith in the sense of barren orthodoxy or assent to doctrinal truth. The only genuine kind of faith is faith that issues in moral conduct. What Paul meant [Romans 4:3-5] by faith, was the spiritual experience of being united to Christ, which is bound, if genuine, to issue in fruitful moral conduct.

SALVATION OBTAINABLE ONLY BY FAITH

Salvation is free. No amount of works can purchase it. It is not for sale. Otherwise a price would be set. That would raise the question, How much does salvation cost? You who are working for salvation——answer *that* question!

As a Jehovah's Witness you are not allowed to accept salvation full and free, but are required to remain in doubt about it for as long as you remain alive. This is not the blessed assurance Christ brought us! This sells you out to the slavery of men. The Christian's faith is in Christ for salvation already obtained for us by Him!

NO J. W. MAY EVER ACCEPT SALVATION FREE

No Christian may ever work for it! The Witnesses quote (out of context, as usual) Philippians 2:12, the part which reads: "Work out your own salvation with fear and trembling." Let us read verses 12 and 13, using *The New Testament* by Charles B. Williams:

So, my dearly beloved friends, as you have always been obedient, so now with reverence and awe keep on working clear down to the finishing point of your salvation, not only as though I were with you but much more because I am away; for it is God Himself who is at work in you to help you desire as well as do it.

Quoting the above from the Weymouth translation, we read:

Therefore my dearly-beloved friends, as I have always found you obedient, labour earnestly with fear and trembling—not merely as though I were present with you, but much more now since I am absent from you—labour earnestly, I say, to make sure of your own salvation. For it is God Himself whose power creates within you both the desire and the power to execute His gracious will.

Again, consider the above passage as rendered by *The Simplified New Testament*:

My beloved, you have always been obedient, not only when I have been with you, but even more so when I have been absent. So now you must demonstrate your own salvation with fear and trembling. It is really God who works in you, so that you are not only willing but also able to carry out His loving purposes.

In finality, consider the rendering of the J. B. Phillips translation:

So then, my dearest friends, as you have always followed my advice—and that not only when I was present to give it—so now that I am far away be keener than ever to work out the salvation that God has given you with a proper sense of awe and responsibility. For it is God who is at work within you, giving you the will and the power to achieve his purpose.

A warning not to reject Jesus Christ is found at Hebrews 12:25, 26, quoting *The Berkeley Version*:

Be careful not to reject the Speaker; for if those people did not escape, who rejected the teacher of God's will on earth, how much less shall we, if we discard the Speaker from heaven. His voice then shook the earth, but now it is announced, "Once more I will shake, not only the earth, but heaven as well."

JUSTICE CALLED—MERCY ANSWERED

"Mercy smiles in the face of judgment" (James 2:13, *Berkeley*). Jehovah's Witnesses are striving vainly toward a second chance for an uncertain salvation that is expected to take a thousand years of human effort to perfect! Whereas true salvation is perfected by, in and through Jesus Christ at the moment one receives Him as personal Saviour.

Paul writes at Romans 5:15-17 according to the J. B. Phillips translation:

> For while as a result of one man's sin death by natural consequence became the common lot of men, it was by the generosity of God, the free giving of the grace of the one man Jesus Christ, that the love of God overflowed for the benefit of all men. Nor is the effect of God's gift the same as the effect of that one man's sin. For in the one case one man's sin brought its inevitable judgment, and the result was condemnation. But, in the other, countless man's sins are met with the free gift of grace, and the result is justification before God.
>
> For if one man's offence meant that men should be slaves to death all their lives, it is a far greater thing that through another man, Jesus Christ, men by their acceptance of his more than sufficient grace and righteousness should live all their lives like kings!

Consider well, Jehovah's Witnesses. When you are willing to lay your all at the foot of the cross, you will be saved. Not until then. You have but one lifetime in which to make that great decision. Not until you come to the end of yourself can you give yourself to the Saviour.

The first step you can make in this direction is to CEASE IMMEDIATELY your futile works performed in sin. You must give up every effort of your own to gain salvation. As long as you hold the slightest price in your hand, He will not accept you. When you have become empty and are ready to accept this free gift from God's hand, then He will become your Father, as you become His son.

Once you have ceased your activities against the gospel, seek Him out in prayer. Open your Bible and read the precious Word, O repentant sinner! On your knees plead the blood of the One Who died because He loved you before you ever loved Him. Kneel at the foot of the cross where He died for *you*! He took your sins and judgment with Him to the cross. Have you no thanks for Him who cleansed your dying soul forever?

Well did Nicodemus ask Jesus "How can these things be?" So Christ stands ready to hear your questioning plea this very moment. In His Word He tells you to come just as you are, right now. He will receive you, and not turn you away.

Would you inquire further into that holy Word? Come, then, for we shall do so!

11

Why I Believe In The Deity Of Christ

IN THE BEGINNING

"In the beginning God created ..." "And God said, Let US make man in OUR image (singular), after OUR likeness (singular) ... So God created man in HIS own IMAGE (singular)" (Genesis 1:1, 26, 27). The Bible does not say that God was speaking to someone else, that is, to someone other than God. Notice how the plural US refers to a singular image and likeness.

When they had built the tower of Babel, God said: "Let US go down, and there confound their language, that they may not understand one another's speech. So THE LORD scattered them abroad ..." (Genesis 11:6, 7). We must allow that "us" means at least two!

And so we read at the very beginning, of a mystery (1 Timothy 3:16). Abraham addressed three men as "Jehovah", and offered to wash his (or *their*?) feet! Read the account at Genesis 18:1-22. The Watch Tower Society says they were all angels. The only clue given as to whether any of them were angels or not is Genesis 19:1, where two angels arrive at Sodom. Compare this with 18:22. If two of them were angels, Abraham had still seen Jehovah! It is very obvious that if they were *all* angels they would have *all* left. Why three angels to *represent* Jehovah? If the one who remained was also an angel, why did the other two leave? And why doesn't the Bible say that this one was also an angel? Why does it indicate he was Jehovah Himself? If this remaining one were simply an angel *representing* Jehovah (as the Watch Tower Society indicates), does this mean that the other two angels were *not* representing Him? Yet, if those three angels *did* re-

142

present Jehovah, why *three* when *one* would have been sufficient? Could Abraham tell the difference between the *representative* angel and the *non-representative* angels?

God told Moses: "Thus shalt thou say unto the children of Israel, I AM (Hebrew, *ehyeh*) hath sent me unto you" (Exodus 3:14). Later on He revealed Himself to Moses by the Divine Name (Exodus 6:3). It is significant that the Son of God also possesses that Divine Name.

JEHOVAH

Jehovah's Witnesses (so-called) are aware of the fact that the pronunciation of the Divine Name has been lost in antiquity. All we have are the four consonants YHWH. This went into Latin as JHVH, and from Latin into English as *Jehovah* through the Tyndale translation.

There are certain descriptions of this Jehovah that the Witnesses are unprepared to accept. One of these is found at Zechariah 2:8-11, quoting here from the *A.S.V.*:

> For thus saith JEHOVAH OF HOSTS: After glory hath HE SENT ME unto the nations which plundered you; for he that toucheth you toucheth the apple of his [Jehovah of hosts'] eye. For behold, I will shake my hand over them, and they shall be a spoil to those that served them; and ye shall know that JEHOVAH OF HOSTS HATH SENT ME. Sing and rejoice, O daughter of Zion; for lo, I (Jehovah) come, and I will dwell in the midst of thee, saith JEHOVAH. And many nations shall join themselves to Jehovah in that day, and shall be my people; and I will dwell in the midst of thee, and thou shalt know that JEHOVAH OF HOSTS HATH SENT ME (Jehovah) unto thee.

The reason the Witnesses cannot accept this portion of Scripture is very obvious: One Jehovah sends another Jehovah in this account! According to them, Jehovah is just *one person*. Here we see where there are two persons, both of whom are Jehovah!

At Zechariah chapter three, one person of Jehovah refers to another Jehovah. Reading verses one and two (*A.S.V.*): "And he showed me Joshua the high priest standing before the angel of Jehovah, and Satan standing at his right hand to be his adversary. And Jehovah said unto Satan, JEHOVAH REBUKE THEE, O Satan; yea, Jehovah that hath chosen Jerusalem rebuke thee ..."

At Isaiah chapter forty-eight Jehovah is sent by the Lord God! In verse twelve He says: "I am the first, I also am the last" (*A.S.V.*). In verse sixteen He says: "Come ye near unto me, hear ye this; from the beginning I have not spoken in secret; from the time that it [the beginning] was, there am I [John 1:1]: and now THE LORD JEHOVAH HATH SENT ME, and his Spirit."

We find at Acts 5:4 that the Holy Spirit is also God; and if God, then He, too is Jehovah. He is sent by the Father, as the Son is sent. So Jehovah sends and is sent; but it is the Father who sends and the Son and Holy Spirit are the sent Ones. No one has seen the person of the Father, but they have seen the Son and the Spirit visibly manifested. All three Persons are Jehovah, the one God. At Isaiah 9:6 the Son is called "Mighty God". Is He a God other than Jehovah? At Deuteronomy 32:39 Jehovah says: "See now that I, even I, am he, and THERE IS NO GOD (*elohim*) WITH ME" (*A.S.V.*). Yet Jesus, referred to as the Word at John 1:1, is said to be eternally "WITH God". The Watch Tower Society translates the end of this verse thus: "The Word was a god" (*New World*). They have "a god" WITH "the God", giving us a big God and a little god, one with the other. It is significant that the word *elohim* is used at Deuteronomy 32:39. This word means *God, gods*, or any object(s) of worship in any rank, position or category, "a god" included!

"THE WORD": WHO IS HE, ACCORDING TO JOHN?

In 1962 the Watch Tower Society printed a booklet attacking the deity of Christ from a theological viewpoint—their first attempt at such, we might add! This booklet was circulated among nearly all the clergy and many of the laity. The exact title is: *The Word: Who Is He? According to John.* At this point we will examine the various accusations against Christ's deity made in this 62-page booklet, confining our study as closely as possible to the subject at hand until we have finished with the booklet. Then we shall proceed beyond that point to complete this chapter.

The main text under consideration is John 1:1, and in particular the Greek words *theos en ho logos*, commonly translated "the Word was God". Moffatt's early translation says "the Logos was God". *The Amplified New Testament* reads "the Word was God Himself". (So also *The New Testament* by Charles B. Williams). *The Concordant Version of the Sacred Scriptures* reads "God was the Word" (word-for-word translation of *theos en ho logos*).* The Watch Tower material argues that if *God* and *Trinity* mean the same thing, then we could conclude that "the Word was with the Trinity" and hence, we would have four Persons. This silly argument is based on the false assumption that the word "God" must always be used in the same manner, with the same breadth of scope, always referring to the *entire* Trinity if there be a Trinity. It ignores the possibility that the word "God" might *sometimes* refer to the entire triune Godhead but at *other times* refer to only one or two Persons of that Godhead. Even as the word "space" can be rightly used of one-dimensional space (distance), of two-dimensional space (area), or of three-dimensional space (volume)—and must be understood according to the context in which it is used—so also the word "God" can properly be used in differing senses. Yes, their assumption is false!—hence their conclusion is false also.

What John 1:1 actually teaches, however, is that the Word, though co-existing *with* the Person God the Father (and, of course, the Holy Spirit too), is *in no sense* any other than a full and equal partaker of Godhead, eternally possessing the full essence and every attribute which belongs to Deity. That is, He is just as truly God as is the Father. (This is what the Greek language structure here reveals, as every learned grammarian knows). The eternal Son is—along with the Father and no less than the Father—part of the Trinity.

Their next argument is that if Christ is not ALL of God, but is one of three Persons, then He is merely one-third God. At first glance the charge may seem accurate and valid. For we readily admit that He is neither God the Father nor God the Holy Spirit, though He and They are identical in divine essence and equally eternal. All three together are God. But no, their charge is false! It cannot be said that He is one-third God (in the way they mean it—quantitatively) any more

*So also reads Martin Luther's Geman translation, and the modern Czech translation (1946) by František Žilka, to mention two others.

than it can be said that length, breadth and height are each one-third (quantitatively) of three-dimensional space. Though these are equal *components* of space, each is not a *third* of space. For though it is possible to speak of them separately (for each is distinct), yet neither length, breadth nor height can exist independently; they cannot be "sliced apart". Each is equally essential to the one indivisible whole. And so it is of the Trinity: three distinct and equal Persons, and yet one God. He cannot be put on a drawing board or on an operating table and dissected into thirds. Rather than insisting that God can be explained on the level of our mentality we must be willing to believe the Biblical description which He gives of Himself. Part of this is found in John 1:1, which tells us that not only was Christ *with* God but that He *was* God. This has to be; otherwise we have a contradiction of Deuteronomy 32:39, where Jehovah says: "There is NO GOD WITH ME." If "a god" (an independent co-Lord of any kind) is *with* God, then there is a contradiction of Scriptures here.

The words of 1 John 5:7, used by many to back up the Trinity doctrine, may or may not be part of the original inspired Word of God. Since we have so much evidence of the Trinity in other portions of the Bible, we will simply ignore this text.

The booklet under discussion says, on page 11: "Search John's writings as much as we can, yet we do not once find that John says that the Word became a God-Man, that is, a combination of God and man." However, note JOHN'S words recorded at John 5:18:

"For this cause therefore the Jews sought the more to kill him, because he not only brake the sabbath, but also called God his own Father, MAKING HIMSELF EQUAL WITH GOD" (*A.S.V.*). And what are Christ's two chief titles? "Son of man" and "Son of God", according to numerical usage. We find "Son of man" mentioned seventy-eight times and "Son of God" used forty-six times in the New Testament (*King James* Bible). He was both. He was God and He was man, even as He was of God and of man.

WAS HE GOD WHILE ON EARTH?

On page 12 of the booklet under discussion the Society brings up the Roman Catholic teaching that Mary was the

146

"mother of God", and ridicules the idea of saying Mary must have been the mother of a third of God, if Jesus is one person of a Trinity. Then they ask: "Who was the father of God? If God had a mother, who was his father?" (page 13). The father of God the *Son* was God the *Father*, the Holy Spirit being used as the instrument to accomplish His birth of Mary (Matthew 1:20). She was the mother of His human nature only; Jesus' divine nature was not received from her.

On page 15, this booklet discusses the "tabernacling" of Christ in the flesh (taught by John 1:14 in the Greek), and compares it with 2 Peter 1:13, 14, *Douay* translation: "I think it meet as long as I am in this tabernacle, to stir you up by putting you in remembrance: being assured that the laying away of my tabernacle is at hand." The Society comments that Peter was not indicating here that he was an incarnation. True; but these words remind us of these: "We are of good courage, I say, and are willing to be absent from the body, and to be at home with the Lord" (2 Corinthians 5:8). That is the *A.S.V.* rendering. Or, as the *King James* Bible reads: " ... willing rather to be absent from the body, and to be present with the Lord." That which can be absent from the body (spoken of here by Paul) is that which tabernacles in the body, spoken of by Peter. So the objection falls apart.

WHAT BELIEVING JEWS CALLED CHRIST

On page 18 the booklet raises the question: "Did the apostles and other disciples get to regarding Jesus as 'God the Son' and calling him such?" Here they broaden the scope beyond the writings of John. We will let the answer to this wait until we complete the discussion of this booklet, confining our material as much as possible to that of John for the present. At this moment we will remind the reader of John 5:18, quoted earlier.

Page 21 brings up their doctrine of the 144,000—i.e., that only that number of the saved will go to heaven. They state that the Bride of Christ will not be married to a third part of a Trinity, or married to God. First of all, let us clear up their erroneous teaching that the Bride is composed of only 144,000 persons. According to Revelation 7:4, these are "sealed out of every tribe of the children of Israel" (*A.S.V.*). Compare this with Romans 11:1-28, where Paul speaks of the restoration of Israel. The 144,000 come into the kingdom established on earth AFTER the return of Christ. They are the first fruits of those who come out of the great tribulation (Revelation 14:4; 7:14).

Page 23 mentions that the Bride is married to the Lamb, not to God the Almighty. Note in Revelation 22:3, however, that there is but ONE throne of God and the Lamb; that They are the ONE temple or sanctuary of the holy city (21:22). Notice in particular these words: "The throne of God and of the Lamb shall be therein: and HIS servants shall serve HIM; and they shall see HIS face; and HIS name [one name of God and the Lamb!] shall be on their foreheads" (Revelation 22:3, 4 *A.S.V.*).

Further, note these words: "And behold, I come quickly. Blessed is he that keepeth the words of the prophecy of this book. I am the Alpha and the Omega, the first and the last, the beginning and the end. I Jesus have sent mine angel to testify unto you these things for the churches. I am the root and offspring of David, the bright, the morning star. He who testifieth these things saith, Yea: I come quickly. Amen: come, Lord Jesus" (Revelation 22:7, 13, 16, 20 *A.S.V.*). At Revelation 1:8 "the Alpha and the Omega" is God (see also 21:6). So John refers to Jesus as God in the Revelation.

SELF-IDENTIFICATION

Under this title the booklet recognizes the text at John 10:33: "For a good work we stone thee not, but for blasphemy; and because thou, being a man, makest thyself God" (*A.S.V.*). Then they quote the next verse, which itself contains a quotation of Psalm 82:6: "Jesus answered them, Is it not written in your law, I said, Ye are gods?" Page 27 comments: "Jesus told those who wanted to stone them that he had not claimed to be God or a god, even though Psalm 82:6 had called some men, some Israelite judges, 'gods'."

The Hebrew word used at Psalm 82:6 is *elohim*, a word with a most interesting and enlightening derivation. Not only does the booklet ignore its true meaning here, but also the fact that it *does* apply to Christ at certain places. You might compare Genesis 1:1 with John 1:3. As regards this particular case, let us see what *A Critical Lexicon and Concord-*

148

ance to the English and Greek Testament by E. W. Bullinger (1957) says. Quoting from pages 896, 897:

As *Logos* is the embodiment and outward expression of the invisible thought, so the 2nd person manifests the invisible Deity, and is said to be "God manifest in the flesh", (1 Tim. iii. 16); "the express image of His person", (Heb. i. 3); "the image of the invisible God", (Col. i. 15.)

The Godhead is "Spirit", (John iv. 24) and as Spirit has no likeness to matter, God himself took some *creature form*, (not human) before He created anything, in order that creation might have a mediator, or a means of communion with Deity. Hence, Christ is said to have been, "In the beginning", (John i. 1); "before all things", (Col. i. 17) The first-born of every creature", (Col. i. 15) "the beginning of the creation of God", (Rev. iii. 14); and hence, "In Him dwelleth all the fulness of the Godhead bodily", (Col. ii. 9).

The *Logos* is therefore God, *i.e. Elohim*. The work of creation is predicated of both, (Gen. i. 1; John i. 3; Col. i. 16; Heb. i. 2.) Elohim is not the title of Deity, but the title of God as the Creator, and always has reference to creation, power, and glory, (while the title "Jehovah" sets forth the self-existent one, and His covenant relationships).

Elohim is the one who was set apart by Deity (so to speak) by an oath for His office in relation to creation. For Alah means to take an oath, and thus the term Elohim is not the title of Deity, but is applied to any who are set apart with the solemnity of an oath to be the representative of another, to carry out certain acts; hence, it is applied not only to the 2nd person of the Trinity, but also to magistrates, (Ex. xxi. 6; xxii. 8, 9, 28, quoted Acts xxiii. 5), to Moses (Ex. vii. 1), and even to Idols, (Ex. xii. 12; Numb. xxv. 2; Gen. xxxi. 30, *cf.* 19) because they were used for representing God. Plural, because *Elohim represents* the Godhead.

Elohim, therefore, is the *Logos* or WORD, who took creaturehood, to create, (as He afterwards took humanity, to redeem). As such He is the Father's "Servant", "Angel", or "Messenger", (*Elohim,* denotes His being set apart to the office with an oath; *Messiah,* or Christ, His anointing to tne work of Redemption; *Angel,* or *Messenger,* referring to His actual dispatch; *Servant*, with reference to the service actually to be done). He appeared to Adam and the Patriarchs, (Gen. xvi., xvii., xviii., xxi., xxii., xxxii.; E. iii., vi.; Josh v. 13-15 (*cf.* Ex. xxiii. 23); Judg. xiii., etc., etc.). This view only makes permanent that which most commentators assume as being only temporary.

His mission in connection with creation was to manifest Deity to His creatures, (Prov. viii. 22-31). His work was begun with Adam (made in His likeness and image), but the fall interrupted that mission, and it was necessarily suspended. Then "the Word was made flesh", (John i. 14) in order that He might redeem the creation from the curse. Made flesh in order that He might suffer and die, (*see* Heb. x. 5; Ps. xl. 6; Is. xlii. 1; Phil. ii. 7).

As the *Logos*, He was "the everlasting Son of the Father", "the only-begotten Son", who was GIVEN. Given to become a human child. Hence, He was "the Son" before He was "a gift", but could not be a human "child" before He was "born" [Isaiah 9:6].

But further, inasmuch as the *Logos*, as the Living Word, became so to manifest and reveal Deity to us, so "the written Word" was given with the same object and for the same purpose. Hence, it is sometimes difficult to know which is intended, as the same things are predicated of each. Both are "*the truth*", (John xiv. 6; xvii. 17). Both are "*everlasting*", (Ps. cxix. 89; Matt. xxiv. 34, 35; 1 Pet. i. 25). Both are "*Life*", (John xi. 25; xiv. 6; 1 Pet. i. 22; 1 John i. 1). Both "*Save*", (Acts xvi. 31; 1 Cor. xv. 2). Both "*Purify*", (Tit. ii. 14; 1 Pet. i. 22). Both "*Sanctify*", (John xvii. 17). Both "*beget to new life*", (1 Pet. i. 23; Jas. i. 18). Both "*shall judge*", (John vi. 26, 27; xii. 48). Both are "*glorified*", (Rom. xv. 9; Acts xiii. 48).

Is this not most enlightening? It certainly does away with many of the Watch Tower Society's false contentions!

THE DISPUTED TEXTS

Part three of the booklet (beginning on page 29) discusses certain texts usually used to prove the deity of Christ and/or the Trinity. One such is John 10:30—"I and my Father are one." The Society says that if the Trinity doctrine were true, then the Father and Son being one would make up two-thirds of the Trinity, not the *entire* Trinity. And somehow, to them, that disproves the Trinity doctrine! This has already been answered in this chapter and will not be repeated here. On page 33 the booklet discusses John 17:3, wherein Jesus calls His Father "the only true God". They state:

> By calling his Father "the only true God" he shut himself out from being God or even a part or a Person of God. Otherwise, the Father would not be the "only true God". The word "only" means, according to the dictionary, "alone in its class; without others of the same class or kind; sole; single; alone, by reason of superiority; pre-eminent; chief". According to Jesus, his Father was, not only the "true God" but also the "only" one. According to his own words, Jesus did not class himself with God.

Yet Jehovah's Witnesses themselves hold that there is more than one "true God"! They believe that Jesus is a "Mighty God" (Isaiah 9:6)—"a god", according to their translation of John 1:1. Would they say now that Jesus is NOT a "true" Mighty God? They believe that Jehovah is *the* true God, and that Jesus is *a* true god! They claim they worship Jehovah but not Jesus; yet, both are true Gods!

Compare this with what we read regarding the "saviour". Reading Isaiah 43:11 (*A.S.V.*): "I, even I, am Jehovah; and besides me there is no saviour." (See also Hosea 13:4). Yet all Jehovah's Witnesses at least verbally give assent to the fact *Jesus* is the Saviour! Yet, according to the texts quoted above, He *cannot* be the Saviour—unless He is Jehovah!

The Society also refers to John 17:21 where Christ prayed to the Father that the believers "may be one in us", and conclude (page 33) that if Christ is God then those believers would become part of the Trinity. However, Christ did *not* pray that the believers would become "one OF us", but rather "one IN us". Note: "in US". Not just "in" the Son but "in" the Father also. Just exactly how are they "one in" *both* the Father and the Son? How can they be equally "in" both? Since the Watch Tower brought up the problem, let them answer it! If the believers are only one "in" these two Persons by reason of the fruits they bear (spiritually), or one in agreement, why doesn't the Bible say this? You see, the Bible teaches a deeper unity and "oneness" than the Jehovah's Witnesses are aware of. And so they explain away these Scriptures to mean merely various expressions of works (which they think they are performing for salvation!)

"I AM"

John 8:58 and Exodus 3:14. The theology of the Watch Tower Society must resist to the bitter end the idea that these texts speak of the same God. For if they do, then that entire theological structure crumbles beyond reconstruction.

The most common rendering of John 8:58 is, "Before Abraham was born, I am." The *King James* rendering of Exodus 3:14 is: "And God said unto Moses, I AM THAT I AM: and he said, Thus shalt thou say unto the children of Israel, I AM hath sent me unto you." Now note how the Watch Tower Bible translates both these texts: "Before Abraham came into existence, I have been" (John 8:58, *N.W.*). "At this point God said to Moses: 'I SHALL PROVE TO BE WHAT I SHALL PROVE TO BE.' And he added: 'This is what you are to say to the sons of Israel, I SHALL PROVE TO BE has sent me to you'" (Exodus 3:14 *N.W.*).

The New World Translation claims its translation of John 8:58 is translated from the Westcott and Hort Greek text. And what is disputed are the Greek words *ego eimi*. The Watch Tower claims that certain translators deliberately translate John 8:58 as "I am", rather than "I am he" as they do at other places, to give us the false idea that Jesus was giving Himself a title that belongs to Jehovah God, in imitation of Exodus 3:14. Notice, however, that while the Watch Tower translation of this expression at John 8:24, 28 is "I am he", at 8:58 it is "I have been". But Christ did NOT use the expression *ego en*—"I was" (or "I have been"). Besides, the next verse states that following these words they picked up stones to stone Him. Why? On the charge of blasphemy— as in the parallel case: "Because thou, being a man, makest thyself God" (John 10:33). If He were merely stating that He existed before Abraham's day, that would not have been saying He was God—the Watch Tower translation freely admits this! Therefore, if Jesus said what the *New World Translation* declares He said, the Jews could NOT have stoned Him on a charge of blasphemy.

The Society states (page 37) that whereas Jesus used *ego eimi*, the *Septuagint* translation of Exodus 3:14 uses *ho ohn* (both usually translated "I am"). So, they argue, the expressions are different and actually have different meanings. But this is a mere evasion of the pertinent facts. And what are the facts?

In Hebrew "I am" is *ehyeh*. *Ehyeh* denotes unconditional existence in ever-active manifestations, and is similar to *Yahweh*—for both are from the root word *hayah* (*A.S.V.* and *R.S.V.* footnotes). The *Septuagint* here renders the Hebrew *ehyeh* as *ho ohn*—the only correct rendering, they imply. However, though in Exodus 3:14 the *Septuagint* does render *ehyeh* two times as *ho ohn*, it also renders it one time as *ego eimi*. And *ego eimi* is the common rendering elsewhere. So it CANNOT be claimed that *ego eimi* is an improper Greek equivalent to the Hebrew word *ehyeh*.

Actually, *ego eimi* (which brings out the linear action) is the consistently better equivalent! As evidence, please note Revelation 1:4, 8; 11:17 and 16:5—the only places in the New Testament where *ho ohn* is applied to God. In these instances it never stands by itself. Why? Because alone it cannot convey the idea of eternal being in ever-active manifestation implied in the Hebrew word *ehyeh*. The Greek *ho ohn* is merely a PORTION of the verbal expression used to designate God. *Ego eimi* conveys the idea more completely. So the Watch Tower argument tries to evade the facts by using this argument upon an inferior *Septuagint* rendering.

The additional contention (page 36), based on the assumption that Jesus spoke to the Jews "in the Hebrew of his day, not in Greek", is also invalid. Two Hebrew translations of John 8:58 are given to supposedly prove that Jesus could not possibly have used the Hebrew *ehyeh* of Exodus 3:14. But I can just as easily refer you to two Hebrew translations in which He *does* say "*ehyeh*". *The Hebrew New Testament* translated from the Greek in 1817 by T. Frey and G. G. Collyer, published by the London Jews Society, reads: " ... *terem yihyeh Abraham ehyeh*"; literally, "before he-came-to-be Abraham, I am". And the *Hebrew New Testament* published by the British and Foreign Bible Society, London, in 1880 has " ... *ani ehyeh*", the emphatic " ... I, I am". Yes, Jesus could have said "*ehyeh*"! So it cannot be shown that Jesus was *not*, as the Watch Tower Society puts it, "trying to imitate Jehovah God and give us the impression that he himself was Jehovah, the I AM". All their objections to this fact fall flat!

INFERIOR?

Next they tackle John 14:9 (on pages 38-40). "He that has seen me has seen the Father." The Society retorts: "No they haven't—they saw only the Son!" Jesus says they *did* see the Father also; the Watch Tower Society says they did not! Now you have a choice of whom you will believe. Here is another case of Watch Tower versus the Bible.

Next they take John 8:28 and the words "I do nothing of myself, but as the Father taught me, I speak these things." He spoke here as a man. But this is the person to whom the Father addressed the words found at Hebrews 1:8: "Thy throne, O God [*ho theos*—THE GOD] is forever and ever." It is true that HO THEOS, "the God", could do nothing of Himself as man (*anthropos*), but as God He was almighty (compare Revelation 22:13, 16 with 1:8). At John 8:28 He spoke as a man.

Next John 6:38, 39 is used to "prove" that Jesus was inferior to God in heaven. Again Jesus is speaking as the Son of man. Remember that John in his Revelation reveals the Father and Son as equal, having the same throne and posessing one name; the same as at Genesis 1:26 where they have but one image and one likeness. He is described at Hebrews 1:3 in the Moffatt 1901 translation as "the reflected radiance of his [the Father's] majesty and the facsimile of his [the Father's] nature". *The Amplified New Testament* reads: "The Light-being, the out-raying of the divine—and He is the perfect imprint and very image of [God's] nature."

The very words that follow those seem to escape Jehovah's Witnesses. Using the *A.S.V.*: "AND UPHOLDING ALL THINGS BY THE WORD OF HIS POWER ..." Moffatt 1901 reads: "Sustaining also all things with the word of his power." *The Amplified New Testament* reads. "Upholding *and* maintaining *and* guiding *and* propelling the universe by His mighty word of power." *The New English Bible* says He "bears along the universe by his word of power" (see footnote). This is the God whom the winds and water must obey (John 17:2). This God made the worlds (Hebrews 1:2).

154

Yes! says the Watch Tower! On page 42 they take to task John 5:23: "That all may honour the Son, even as they honour the Father" (*A.S.V.*). According to *The New English Bible* this verse reads: "It is his will that all should pay the same honour to the Son as to the Father. To deny honour to the Son is to deny it to the Father who sent him." Here equal honour is plainly taught in Scripture.

Further we read in verse 26: "For as the FATHER HATH LIFE IN HIMSELF, even so gave he to the SON ALSO TO HAVE LIFE IN HIMSELF" (*A.S.V.*). Both Father and Son have life in themselves; as the Father is uncreated, so the Son likewise. Reading *The Amplified New Testament*: "For even as the Father has life in Himself *and* is self-existent, so He has given to the Son to have life in Himself *and* be self-existent." As John 1:4 states, "In him was life". And so, "He that hath the Son hath LIFE" (1 John 5:12).

The booklet states on page 44: "Jesus' own continuance in life depended on his obedience to God his Father." In other words, if He stops being obedient, then His life comes to an end! Yet consider these words of contradiction to this: "NO ONE TAKETH IT AWAY FROM ME" (John 10:18, *A.S.V.*)! Referring to His coming crucifixion He adds: "I LAY IT DOWN OF MYSELF!" The Watch Tower says someone could have taken Jesus' life; Jesus says no one could take His life away. Once again, whom will you believe— Watch Tower or the Bible? Make your choice now.

On page 45 the Society acknowledges Christ's title of "the First and the Last" as recorded at Revelation 1:17, 18. They conclude He was merely "the first and last in the matter of resurrection ... the first one on earth that God raised from the dead to be 'alive for evermore'. He is also the last one whom God raises thus directly ..." They fail to make mention of the fact that He is also "the Alpha and the Omega" and "the beginning and the end" (Revelation 22:13). This is Almighty God at Revelation 21:6 and 1:8. Compare these texts with Isaiah 44:6 and 48:12.

REVELATION 3:14

They have always used this text to support their idea that Jesus was created; He was, they say, the beginning of all creation. Their translation of this text reads, "The beginning of the creation by God". Now take note of these words found on page 47: "AT HIS RESURRECTION JESUS CHRIST WAS GOD'S CREATION OR A CREATION BY GOD" (Emphasis mine.) At the top of page 48 they say: "But at the very beginning of all creation Jesus was God's creation, a creature produced by God." Not all are aware of the fact that the Watch Tower Society teaches that Jesus was CREATED TWICE! But that they do teach, indeed!

Note the following translations of Revelation 3:14:

These are the words of the Amen, the trusty *and* faithful and true Witness, the Origin *and* Beginning *and* Author of God's creation. [Is. 55:4; Prov. 8:22.]
(*The Amplified New Testament*).

These are the words of the Amen, the faithful and true witness, the prime source of all God's creation (*New English Bible*).

These things saith the Amen, the faithful and true witness, the origin of God's creation (Moffatt, 1901).

These are the words of the Amen, the faithful and true witness, the origin of God's creation (Moffatt, 1922).

Thus speaks the Amen, the Faithful and True Witness, the Origin of God's creation (*The Simplified New Testament* by Olaf M. Norlie).

Note in John 17:5 that the glory which Jesus was to receive following His resurrection was the SAME GLORY He had with His Father before He came to earth—which glory the Father said would not be shared with anyone (Isaiah 42:8). Note, in this instance also, Hebrews 1:10, 11 compared with Psalms 102:24-27 from which it is quoted. Here Christ is immutable as is the Father. If He is immutable, then He indeed is God without question. According to Hebrews 13:8 Christ IS immutable—"the same yesterday, today and forever!" Compare this with Malachi 3:6—"I, Jehovah, change not!"

See also James 1:17.

JOHN 20:28

Here Thomas says to Christ (*autou*) "My Lord and my

156

God!" From pages 48 to 51 the booklet discusses this problem, which is a thorny one among Jehovah's Witnesses. In this text Thomas addresses Christ as *ho Theos*—"the God". On page 50 this booklet asks: "How, then, could Thomas in an ecstasy of joy at seeing the resurrected Jesus for the first time burst out with an exclamation and speak to Jesus himself as being the one and only living, true God, the God whose name is Jehovah?" What they seem to deliberately fail to recognize here is that Thomas addressed these words to JESUS, recognizing Him as God the Son, not making him out to be God the Father. The Father Himself addresses Jesus by this title at Hebrews 1:8, and so Christ commended Thomas on his belated acknowledgment (John 20:29).

Concerning this event we quote here from *Matthew Henry's Commentary* (1 Vol., Zondervan Publishing House, Grand Rapids; Marshall, Morgan & Scott, London; 1960.) from page 1629:

(1) Thomas is now fully satisfied of the truth of Christ's resurrection. His slowness and backwardness to believe may help to strengthen our faith.

(2) He therefore believed him to be the Lord and God, and we are to believe him so. [1] We must believe his deity —that he is God; not a man made God, but God made man. [2] His mediation—that he is Lord, the one Lord, to settle the great concerns that lie between God and man, and to establish the correspondence that was necessary to our happiness. (3) He consented to him as his Lord and his God. We must accept of Christ to be that to us which the Father hath appointed him. This is the vital act of faith, He is mine.

On page 51 the Watch Tower booklet brings them right into the jaws of a trap they had set for others. They state:

So if Thomas addressed Jesus as "my God", Thomas had to recognize Jesus' Father as the God of a God, hence as a God higher than Jesus Christ, a God whom Jesus himself worshipped.

IF Jesus is some OTHER God than Jehovah, then indeed we DO have "the God of a God"! BUT—if Jesus is ALSO Jehovah, then we have but ONE GOD in the Persons of the

Father, Son *and* Holy Spirit. The Watch Tower Society teaches that there are two Gods—an Almighty God and a mighty God; the Almighty God is supposed to have created the mighty God. They are supposed to be a Father-and-son-God team.

Now on page 51 this booklet closes part 4 by referring to Revelation chapter four, verses 1-11 and "a symbolic description of this God, the 'Lord God Almighty', who sits upon the heavenly throne and who lives for ever and ever". Then on to chapter five, verses 5-8 for a description of "Jesus Christ as the Lamb of God who comes to the Lord God Almighty on his throne ...." Let us now study portions of these two chapters and see what we can learn therefrom in contrast to what has just been quoted from the booklet.

REVELATION FOUR AND FIVE

It is now proposed to show herein where Jehovah's Witnesses have so greatly erred in their Arian teaching concerning Jesus Christ. We shall use the standard *King James* Bible here, but the reader is urged to read these passages from newer translations which may aid in an even clearer understanding of these great truths. We shall show the parallel teachings of chapters four and five and what they clearly prove.

CHAPTER FOUR	CHAPTER FIVE
And around about the throne were four and twenty seats; and upon the seats I saw four and twenty elders sitting. (Verse 4).	And one of the elders saith. . . Weep not: behold, the Lion of the tribe of Juda. . . hath prevailed to open the book. (Verse 5).

Now we have the scene of twenty-four elders seated round the throne, clothed in white and wearing gold crowns; one speaks to John and tells him the book will be opened by One worthy.

CHAPTER FOUR	CHAPTER FIVE
And there were seven lamps of fire burning before the throne, which are the seven Spirits of God. (Verse 5).	And I beheld . . . in the midst of the throne . . . a Lamb as it had been slain, having seven horns and seven eyes, which are the seven Spirits of God . . . (Verse 6).

158

Notice now, the seven lamps of fire (4:5) are the seven Spirits of God. The Lamb has seven horns and seven eyes (5:6) which are the seven Spirits of God. The Lamb, of course, is Jesus Christ.

CHAPTER FOUR	CHAPTER FIVE
And in the midst of the throne, and round about the throne, were four beasts full of eyes before and behind. (Verse 6).	And when he (the Lamb) had taken the book, the four beasts and four and twenty elders fell down before the Lamb . . . (Verse 8).

Here we behold a sea like crystal before the throne, and in the midst four beasts (4:6). In verse seven, chapter five, the Lamb takes the book from him that sat on the throne, and the four beasts and twenty-four elders then fall before the Lamb (5:8).

Now we come to the meatier part of the story:

CHAPTER FOUR	CHAPTER FIVE
And when those beasts give glory . . . to him that sat on the throne . . . the four and twenty elders fall down before him that sat on the throne, and worship him that liveth for ever and ever, and cast their crowns before the throne . . . (Verses 9, 10).	And the four beasts and twenty elders fell down and worshipped him that liveth for ever and ever. (Verse 14). I am he that liveth, and was dead . . . I am alive for evermore. (1:18; 2:8).

Perhaps the reader has yet to grasp the significance of what is written here. Therefore let us make the following comparison of Scriptures:

CHAPTER FOUR	CHAPTER FIVE
The four and twenty elders fall down before him that sat on the throne . . . (Verse 10).	The four beasts and four and twenty elders fell down before THE LAMB . . . (Verse 8).
Thou art worthy, O Lord, to receive glory and honour and power: for thou hast created all things, and for thy pleasure they are and were created. (Verse 11).	Worthy is THE LAMB that was slain to receive power, and riches, and wisdom, and strength, and honour, and glory, and blessing. (Verse 12). All things were made by him (John 1:3). For by him were all things created . . . all things were created by him and for him (Colossians 1:16).

Now we give full evidence that the Christ (the Lamb) is NOT simply a creature:

<table>
<tr><td>CHAPTER FOUR</td><td>CHAPTER FIVE</td></tr>
<tr><td>And the four beasts . . . rest not day and night, saying, Holy, holy, holy, Lord God Almighty, which was, and is, and is to come. (Verse 8).</td><td>And every creature which is in heaven, and on the earth . . . heard I saying, Blessing, and honour, and glory, and power, be unto him that sitteth upon the throne, and unto the Lamb for ever and ever. (Verse 13).</td></tr>
</table>

You see, the Lamb is contrasted with every creature (5:13) which comes to worship before the throne. If He were simply a creature, then He, too, would be worshipping with the others. But He (the Lamb) worships NOT before the throne. Rather, He receives the very same homage and adoration that is given to Him who sits upon the throne. For, as we have already noticed (4:10; 5:8), the beasts and twenty-four elders bow in worship to both God the Father and the Lamb. Perhaps this will shed some light of understanding upon John 5:23.

Now once again let us draw a comparison of texts: "Holy, holy, holy, Lord God Almighty which was, and is, and is to come" (Revelation 4:8). "I am the Alpha and the Omega, the beginning and the ending, saith the Lord, which is, and which was, and which is to come, the Almighty" (Revelation 1:8). Now let us note the similar titles and promised return of Jesus Christ:

And behold, I come quickly . . . I am Alpha and Omega, the beginning and the end, the first and the last . . . I Jesus have sent mine angel to testify unto you these things in the churches. I am the root and the offspring of David, and the bright and morning star. . . . He which testifieth these things saith, Surely I come quickly. (Revelation 22:12, 13, 16, 20.)

Note further that "the Lord God Almighty and the Lamb are the temple" of the holy city (Revelation 21:22). The two compose ONE temple. Note also, that the one throne is "the throne of God and of the Lamb" (22:1, 3). Note very carefully: "The throne of God and of the Lamb shall be in it; and HIS servants shall serve HIM: And they shall see HIS face; and HIS NAME shall be in their foreheads" (22:3, 4). What is this one unique name? Could it be "Jehovah"?

And now we proceed to the conclusion of this particular subject under discussion.

BACK TO JOHN 1:1, 2

They begin the final portion of the booklet (page 52) with quotations from 1 John, and in particular we note their rendering of chapter five, verse eighteen: "We know that every [person] that has been born from God does not practice sin, but the One born from God watches him ..." They use "the One born from God" as evidence that Christ was created. This rendering is from their own translation, of course. Let us read this same text from *other* translations:

> We know that whosoever is begotten of God sinneth not; but he that was begotten of God keepeth himself (footnote: Or, "him") ... *A.S.V.*
> We know that no child of God is a sinner; it is the Son of God who keeps him safe ... *The New English Bible.*
> Finally, we know that anyone born of God will not practice sin. For the Son of God will guard him ... *The Simplified New Testament* (Norlie).
> We know that whoever is a child of God is not habitually committing sin; but he who is God's child guards himself ... (Montgomery).
> We know that every one who has been begotten by God does not sin; but the one begotten by God guards himself ... *The Emphatic Diaglott.*
> We know that no one who has received the new life from God lives in sin. No, he who has received the new life from God keeps the thought of God in his heart ... *The Twentieth Century New Testament.*
> No one who has become part of God's family makes a practice of sinning, for Christ, God's Son, holds him securely ... *Living Letters* (Taylor).

This booklet now states on page 53:

> Certainly the apostle John was not so unreasonable as to say that someone ("the Word") was with some other indi-

vidual ("God") and at the same time was that other individual ("God").

We reply with Deuteronomy 32:39: "See now that I, even I, am he, and there is no god with me." We await the Watch Tower Society to now prove that this text does not mean what it says, as they have done with so many others! Further on page 53 they state: "Note that his name is not called 'God the Word', but is called 'The Word of God', or God's Word." We reply with John 1:1 as found in the *Concordant Version of the Sacred Scriptures* (1930):

In the beginning was the Word, and the Word was toward God, AND GOD WAS THE WORD.

Nor does this translation stand alone; notice footnote on page 145.

On page 55 a quotation from C. F. D. Moule is made. They overlook the fact that what he says therein contradicts their "a god" theory. Quoting this portion:

It would be pure Sabellianism to say "the Word was *ho theos*". No idea of inferiority of nature is suggested by the form of expression, which simply affirms the TRUE DEITY OF THE WORD (Emphasis mine).

Then on page 56 they go back to their childishness again —pulling the old trick of quoting John 1:1 from *The Emphatic Diaglott*: "And the LOGOS was with GOD, and the LOGOS was God." In this manner they try to sell the Witnesses the idea that the Word is a god inferior to the Father.

Pages 56-59 are spent on "proving" that Christ is one among many *elohim*, or "sons of God". They indicate (page 58) that the Jews accepted the idea of many *elohim* while still believing in one God. However, if you ask a J. W. to start naming some Gods, he does not go very far. Ask him how many Gods (or "gods") he recognizes, and he will tell you, "Just one—Jehovah!" He claims to recognize Jesus as "a god", but he does not worship him. So in the final tally he will admit to believing in a big God (Jehovah) and a little god (Jesus). These are the Jehovah's Witnesses *elohim*. He also accepts Satan as a god, but not over himself, of course!

162

Now note this statement on page 59:

Certainly the Word or Logos, whom God his Father used in bringing into existence all other creatures, was the chief of the firstborn among ALL THE OTHER ANGELS whom the Hebrew Scriptures call *elohim* or "gods". (Emphasis mine.)

To which we reply:

For to which of the angels did (God) ever say, You are My son, today I have begotten You [that is, established You in an official Sonship relation, with kingly dignity]? And again, I will be to Him a Father, and He be to Me a Son? [Ps. 2:7; II Sam. 2:14.]—*The Amplified New Testament*. (Hebrews 1:5).

For God NEVER SAID TO ANY ANGEL, "Thou art my Son; today I have begotten thee", or again, "I will be father to him, and he shall be my son". *The New English Bible*. (Hebrews 1.5).

For God NEVER SAID TO ANY ANGEL, "You are my Son, and today I have given you the honour that goes with that Name". *Living Letters, The Paraphrased Epistles* by Kenneth N. Taylor. (Hebrews 1:5).

The booklet closes with a final slam against the deity of Christ, under "THE WORD". Say they: "His very title 'The Word' marks him as the Chief One among the sons of God" (page 59). To which we reply:

God loved the world so much that he gave his ONLY [*monogenes*] SON . . . —*New English Bible*. (John 3:16). See also *The New Testament* by Charles B. Williams; Moffatt (both 1901 and 1922); Weymouth; *The Twentieth Century New Testament*.

Either Jesus *is* God's ONLY SON (that is, a Son that is God like Himself), or He *isn't*. Here again we have the Watch Tower in collision with the Bible. Choose sides whom you will serve.

And now we go on to see what the Scriptures beyond those recorded by John teach about the deity of Jesus Christ.

Jesus is God the Saviour, according to Paul at Titus 1:3, 4; 2:10. Then at Colossians 2:9 we have that text which the Watch Tower Society had to change. Their rendering according to the Watch Tower Bible (1961 edition) reads: "Because it is in him that all the fullness of the divine quality dwells bodily." We now compare that with the following translations:

For it is in Christ that the complete being of the Godhead dwells embodied (*New English Bible*).

For in Him all the fulness of the Godhead dwells bodily (Berkeley).

For in Him the whole fulness of Deity (the Godhead), continues to dwell in bodily form—giving complete expression of the divine nature (*The Amplified New Testament*).

For it is in Christ that the fulness of God's nature dwells embodied (Weymouth).

Because in him dwells all the fullness of the Deity bodily (*The Emphatic Diaglott*).

For in Christ the Godhead in all its fulness dwells incarnate (*The Twentieth Century New Testament*).

For in him is embodied and dwells the fullness of the Godhead (*The New Testament*, James Kleist and Joseph Lilly).

Know this, that in Christ all the fulness of the Godhead dwells bodily (*The Simplified New Testament*, Olaf M. Norlie).

For it is in Him that all the fullness of Deity continues to live embodied (*The New Testament*, Charles B. Williams).

Seeing that in Him the entire complement of the Deity dwells bodily (*The Concordant Version of the Sacred Scriptures*).

For it is in Christ that all the fulness of deity dwells bodily (*The New Testament in Modern English*, Montgomery).

For it is in him that all the fulness of the Deity dwells bodily (Moffatt, 1901).

It is in Christ that the entire Fulness of deity has settled bodily (Moffatt, 1922).

For in Christ there is all of God in a human body (*Living Letters*, Kenneth N. Taylor).

Concerning Christ, Paul says at Colossians 1:16 (*American Standard Version*):

For in him were all things created, in the heavens and upon the earth, things visible and things invisible, whether thrones or dominions or principalities or powers; all things have been created through him, and unto him.

Then, lest any should think (like Jehovah's Witnesses do) that He Himself was created as a part of this creation just described, verse 17 states: "AND HE IS BEFORE ALL THINGS."

HEBREWS

Christ was called to be a priest "after the order of Melchizedec" (Hebrews 5:10). He has "neither beginning of days nor end of life" (7:3). Christ is a priest for ever after this order (7:17). His priesthood is unchangeable (7:24). He is "the God" (*ho theos*)—Hebrews 1:8.

BRINGING THE WHOLE TOGETHER

This discussion would not be complete without including the deity and personality of the Holy Spirit. He also is God. The Watch Tower Society teaches that the Holy Spirit is "active force" only—*not* a person. However, only a person could do what the Bible ascribes to the Holy Spirit. At John 14:26 and 15:26 the Bible uses the masculine gender *ekeinos* rather than the neuter gender *ekeino*, thus giving personality to the Holy Spirit. In the following Scriptures the Spirit bears witness to the adoption of believers: Romans 8:16; Galatians 4:6; 1 John 3:24; 4:13; 5:6. In these texts He is the Teacher: Nehemiah 9:20; Luke 12:12; John 14:26; 1 Corinthians 2:13; 1 John 2:27. One can sin against the Holy Spirit: Isaiah 63:10; Matthew 12:31; Mark 3:29; Acts 5:3; Ephesians 4:30; 1 Thessalonians 5:19.

The Holy Spirit guides into all truth (John 16:13); controls movements of believers (acts 1;:19, 20); directs in the selection of leaders (Acts 13:2); He chooses the field of operation (Acts 16:6); He gives life (John 6:63; Romans 8:11; 2 Corinthians 3:6; 1 Peter 3:18); He brings to remembrance (John

165

14:26); He convicts the world of sin (John 16:7, 8); He sanctifies (1 Peter 1:2).

In short, He is a divine Person!

We know of no better way of describing the Scriptural unity among the Persons of the Godhead than that given in the Athanasian Creed. So we quote here in full the translation by Theodore G. Tappert, from *The Book of Concord* (Muhlenberg Press, Philadelphia, 1959):

Whoever wishes to be saved must, above all else, hold the true Christian faith. Whoever does not keep it whole and undefiled will without doubt perish for eternity.

This is the true Christian faith, that we worship one God in three persons and three persons in one God,

without confusing the persons or dividing the divine substance.

For the Father is one person, the Son is another, and the Holy Spirit is still another,

but there is one Godhead of the Father and of the Son and of the Holy Spirit, equal in glory and coequal in majesty.

What the Father is, that is the Son and that is the Holy Spirit:

the Father is uncreated, the Son is uncreated, the Holy Spirit is uncreated;

the Father is unlimited, the Son is unlimited, the Holy Spirit is unlimited;

the Father is eternal, the Son is eternal, the Holy Spirit is eternal;

and yet they are not three eternals but one eternal,

just as there are not three who are uncreated and who are unlimited, but there is one who is uncreated and unlimited.

Likewise the Father is almighty, the Son is almighty, the Holy Spirit is almighty,

and yet there are not three who are almighty but there is one who is almighty.

So the Father is God, the Son is God, the Holy Spirit is God,

and yet they are not three Gods but one God.

So the Father is Lord, the Son is Lord, the Holy Spirit is Lord, and yet they are not three Lords but one Lord.

For just as we are compelled by Christian truth to acknowledge each person by himself to be God and Lord,

so we are forbidden by the Christian religion to say that there are three Gods or three Lords.

The Father was neither made nor created nor begotten by anybody.

The Son was not made or created, but was begotten by the Father.

The Holy Spirit was not made or created or begotten, but proceeds from the Father and the Son.

Accordingly there is one Father and not three Fathers, one Son and not three Sons, one Holy Spirit and not three Holy Spirits.

And among these three persons none is before or after another, none is greater or less than another,

but all three persons are coequal and coeternal, and accordingly, as has been stated above, three persons are to be worshipped in one Godhead and one God to be worshipped in three persons.

Whoever wishes to be saved must think thus about the Trinity.

It is also necessary for eternal salvation that one faithfully believe that our Lord Jesus Christ became man,

for this is the right faith, that we believe and confess that our Lord Jesus Christ the Son of God, is at once God and man:

he is God, begotten before the ages of the substance of the Father, and he is man, born in the world of the substance of his mother,

perfect God and perfect man, with reasonable soul and human flesh,

equal to the Father with respect to his Godhead and inferior to the Father with respect to his manhood.

Although he is God and man, he is not two Christs but one Christ:

one, that is to say, not by changing the Godhead into flesh but by taking on the humanity into God,

one, indeed, not by confusion of substance but by unity in one person.

For just as the reasonable soul and the flesh are one man, so God and man are one in Christ, who suffered for our salvation, descended into hell, rose from the dead,

ascended into heaven, is seated on the right hand of the Father, whence he shall come to judge the living and the dead.

At his coming all men shall rise with their bodies and give an account of their own deeds.

Those who have done good will enter eternal life, and those who have done evil will go into everlasting fire.

This is the true Christian faith. Unless a man believe this firmly and faithfully, he cannot be saved.

THE AGE-OLD DENIAL

Heretics have always denied the Trinity and, in particular, the deity of Christ. Quoting *The Early Days of Christianity* by F. W. Farrar (1889) under "The Growth of Heresy" on page 494:

There were, as I have said, three great events which deeply influenced the last and most active period in the life of St. John—the Neronian persecution, the fall of Jerusalem, and the growth of Heresy.... The third event was very gradual.... According to the tradition of the Church, they [John's letters to the seven churches] were especially written to combat heresy, not by the method of direct and vehement controversy, but by that noblest of all methods which consists in the irresistible presentation of counter truths.

That is the method the writer has attempted to use in this book. Quoting the above source again, this time from page 495:

The *moral* fibre of bitterness, from which all heresies spring, is one and the same. Whether they result from the blind and tyrannous unanimity of corrupt Churches, or the wide self-assertion of opinionated individuals, they owe their ultimate origin to the pride and ambition of the heart.

Now getting specific regarding those heretics who denied Jesus' deity. From page 500:

168

The name of Cerinthus is mixed up with fantastic legends; but the accounts given of his views are full of uncertainty and contradiction, seem to show that he was one of those who "wavered like a wave of the sea", and was tossed about by every wind of doctrine.

Quoting now from *History of Christian Doctrine* by George Park Fisher (1897), page 56:

He [Cerinthus] derived his ideas from Alexandria, but came to Asia Minor, where he was a contemporary of the Apostle John. He represented the Supreme God as utterly separate from any immediate relation to matter. Between them are ranks of angels, one of whom, in a lower grade, was the maker of the world and the God of the Jews.

Such was one of the early heretics who vehemently denied the deity of Jesus Christ. From his thinking and those of others like him, there came to be what is now known as Arianism; named from the one who developed this creature-Christ theory—Arius. Quoting from *History of the Christian Church* by George Crooks and John Hurst (1897), Volume 1, beginning on page 431:

The Arian controversy, the first in the long series, turned upon what has been recognized in all times as the central fact of Christianity, the divinity of Jesus Christ. Its scene was Alexandria, Palestine, and Constantinople. Its chief sources lay in the vague teachings of the Antiochian school and the incongruities of the theology of Origen. It had played an important part in the heresies of the Ebionites, of Artemon and Theodotus.... There can be no greater error, however, than to suppose that the Arian controversy affected only the one doctrine of the divinity of Christ. At every stage of its progress it bore upon the whole divine nature of the Godhead.

Quoting now from the same source, page 432:

The issue between Arius and his bishop was clearly defined.... The orthodox, as represented by Alexander, claimed, first, that his [Christ's] generation was from eternity, and hence coeval [co-eternal] with the Father; and second, that the Son was so derived of and from the father that he was of the same essence with the Father. Both these doctrines were denied by Arius and his followers.

Alexander, failing to convince him of his error, summoned a synod, which met at Alexandria in 321 and condemned the opinions of Arius and deposed him from his office.

The controversy raged; Athanasius (a proponent of the Trinity) was banished by Constantine. The Arians had their troubles, too. The above quoted book says, page 437:

Arianism, like the forms of deviation from evangelical standards in every age, had its weakness in an inherent want of unity. Error is never at one with itself. The Arians became divided immediately after their defeat at Nicea. Failure instead of uniting them, exposed their defects and subjected them to conflicting interests. In addition to the Arianism which first appeared at Alexandria there were two general tendencies, one toward a compromise with Alexandrian orthodoxy and the other toward schism and radical Unitarianism.

For a period of considerable length the Arian tendencies had been extremely popular in Constantinople. It was the battle ground where orthodoxy and heresy had free scope. The city itself being remote from the atmosphere of Alexandria and the personal influence of Athanasius, and Arianism having so many adherents in full confidence of the imperial head, the scales were often equally balanced between truth and error. But many of the Gothic barbarians were then in the city, and they generally adopted the views of Arius. Chrysostom preached against it, but his eloquence and zeal had little effect on the barbarian portion of the population.

Near the close of the sixth century, in the year 589, the only people of Arian preference were the Lombards.

Now once again the Arians have arisen and cause many to stumble. All the cults deny the deity of Christ. They disagree with one another about Christ; but on this one thing they are agreed—he is *not* God!

And we know that Christ, God's Son, has come to help us understand and to find the true God. And now we are in God because we are in Jesus Christ His Son, Who is the only true God; and He is eternal Life. (1 John 5:20— *Living Letters, The Paraphrased Epistles*, Kenneth Taylor.)

12

Why I Believe In The Life Hereafter

DENIAL BY THE WATCHTOWER

Jehovah's Witnesses deny the immaterial soul and teach instead the following, taken from *Make Sure of All Things*, page 349:

> A soul, heavenly or earthly, is a living, sentient (or sense-possessing, conscious, intelligent) creature or person. A soul, heavenly or earthly, consists of a body together with the life principle or life force actuating it. An earthly soul is a living, breathing, sentient creature, animal or human. Earthly souls, human and animal, have an organism of flesh kept living by means of blood circulating in their system.

Also, according to Jehovah's Witnesses, hell is not a place of conscious punishment for the wicked, but is simply the grave. Quoting the above book on page 154:

> False religion teaches that hell is a place where the wicked suffer a twofold punishment: the pain of loss and the pain of sense.... This unreasonable doctrine contradicts the Bible....

It is true that in some cases (particularly the Old Testament) *soul* is simply the living creature, and *sheol* (hell) is the place of burial. But not always. It is these *other* portions of Scripture to which we would like to direct the attention of the reader at this time.

We are not going to prove the existence of a soul merely to prove the existence of hell. One hears it said from time to time: "Jesus spoke more about hell than He did of heaven!" This is simply not so. Jesus referred to hell (using both *hades* and *gehenna*) fourteen times. But He spoke of heaven some eighty-one times!* At this point let us see where the souls of the righteous rest in heaven after the death of their human bodies.

We have read Revelation 6:9-11:

And when he had opened the fifth seal, I saw under the altar THE SOULS OF THEM THAT WERE SLAIN for the word of God, and for the testimony which they held. And they [the souls of the slain] cried with a loud voice, saying, How long, O Lord, holy and true, dost thou not judge and avenge our blood on them that dwell on the earth? And white robes were given unto every one of them [the souls of the slain]; and it was said unto them, that they should REST yet for a little season, until their fellow-servants also and their brethren, THAT SHOULD BE KILLED AS THEY WERE, should be fulfilled.

Consider also these words recorded at Revelation 20:4:

And I saw thrones, and they sat upon them, and judgment was given unto them: AND I SAW THE SOULS OF THEM THAT WERE BEHEADED for the witness of Jesus, and for the word of God. . . .

That is why we read at Matthew 10:28:

And be not afraid of them that kill the body, BUT ARE NOT ABLE TO KILL THE SOUL: but rather fear him who is able to destroy BOTH soul and body in Gehenna (*A.S.V.*, footnote).

By giving Genesis 2:7 a casual reading the J. W. thinks that the flesh and *blood* is the entire soul. The answer to this is well put in a tract by Robert M. Delancy. Quoting a portion:

*Source: Young's *Analytical Concordance.*

173

Let us consider Genesis 2:7. In this and other similar passages the word "soul" clearly refers to the entire person or individual. This we readily admit. Many modern translations support this fact. " ... man became a living being" (*R.S.V., Moffatt, Confraternity, An American Translation* (Goodspeed), and *Lamsa*); yes, an entire person is often called a soul—"My, you're a restless soul," etc. Man very definitely *is* a soul; but he "is a soul" expressly because he does "have a soul".

The use of the word "soul" for the entire individual is simply a *synecdoche,* a common figure of speech in which the name of the most important part of a thing is applied to the entire object. Thus a woman may speak of purchasing "a pair of heels", meaning a pair of high-heeled shoes. A mariner may call out, "I see five sails", meaning not sails alone but five sailboats. A tourist may rave about the mighty peaks in Switzerland, but he has reference to the entire mountains, not just their peaks. Or we may speak of autumn as "fall", not because the falling of leaves occurs every day of the season or is its only activity, but because this is the *most important* event of the season. And referring to the entire individual as a soul, since it is truly his most important part, is simply another use of *synecdoche* —a figure of speech found in nearly all languages from earliest times.

PUNISHMENT BEYOND PHYSICAL DEATH?

Consider these words recorded at Hebrews 10:28, 29 from the following translations:

He that despised Moses' law died without mercy under two or three witnesses: Of how much sorer punishment, suppose ye, shall he be thought worthy, who hath trodden under foot the Son of God, and hath counted the blood of the covenant, wherewith he was sanctified, an unholy thing, and hath done despite unto the Spirit of grace? (*King James*).

Any one who bids defiance to the Law of Moses is put to death without mercy on the testimony of two or three witnesses. How much severer punishment, think you, will be held to deserve who has trampled under foot the Son of God, has not regarded as holy that Covenant-blood with which he was set free from sin, and has insulted the Spirit from which comes grace? (*Weymouth*).

When a man disregarded the Law of Moses, he was, on the evidence of two or three witnesses, put to death without pity, How much WORSE [than physical death] then, think you, will be the punishment deserved by those who have trampled underfoot the Son of God, who have treated the blood that rendered the Covenant valid—the very blood by which they were purified—as of no account, and who have outraged the Spirit of Love? (*Twentieth Century New Testament*).

When a man defies the laws of Moses, and is convicted of this by two or three witnesses, he has to die without hope of mercy. How much worse is that man who has trampled the Son of God under foot, who has valued as worthless the blood of the covenant by which he had his sins forgiven, and who has insulted the Spirit of Grace! Will not such a one be counted worthy of a punishment even more severe [than death without mercy]? (*The Simplified New Testament*).

A man who refused to obey the laws given by Moses was killed without mercy if there were two or three witnesses to his sin. Think how much more terrible the punishment will be for those who have trampled underfoot the Son of God and treated His cleansing blood as though it were common and unhallowed, thus insulting and outraging the Holy Spirit Who brings God's mercy to His people (*Living Letters*, Kenneth N. Taylor).

SHEOL, HADES, GEHENNA

Consider what Deuteronomy 32:22 says: "For a fire is kindled in mine anger, and shall burn unto the lowest hell [sheol], and shall consume the earth with her increase, and set on fire the foundations of the mountains." If *sheol* is just an ordinary grave, what is meant by the *lowest* sheol reached by fire? Charles Thomson's translation of the Greek *Septuagint* reads: "Since a fire is kindled because of my wrath, it shall burn down to the lowest Hades; it shall consume the land, and the products thereof; it shall set on fire the foundations of the mountains." Rotherham's translation reads: "For a fire is kindled in mine anger, and shall burn AS FAR AS hades beneath, and consume the earth with her produce, and set ablaze the foundations of the mountains." If *sheol* or *hades* is just six feet under, why does the text say "as far as hades beneath"? Plainly, this indicates more than the body descending into the grave.

Again, let us consider Psalm 86:13: "For great is thy mercy toward me: and thou hast delivered my soul from the lowest hell." Thomson reads: "For thy mercy to me hath been great; Thou hast delivered my soul from the deepest mansion of the dead." The *A.S.V.*: "For great is thy loving kindness toward me; And thou hast delivered my soul from the lowest Sheol."

Consider Psalms 116:3 (*A.S.V.*): "The cords of death compassed me, and the pains of Sheol found me." If there is no soul or life after the body dies, how could the "pains of Sheol" follow physical death? Again, *death* and *Sheol* are separate at Proverbs 5:5, *A.S.V.*: "Her feet go down to death; her steps take hold on Sheol." Rotherham reads: "Her feet are going down to death,—on hades will her steps take firm hold."

Read now Proberbs 9:18 (*A.S.V.*): "But he knoweth not that the dead (*shades*, footnote) are there; that her guests are in the depths of Sheol." *The Amplified Old Testament* reads: "But he knows not that the shades of the dead are there [spectres haunting the scene of past transgressions], and that her invited guests are [already sunk] in the depths of Sheol —the lower world, Hades."

Look at these words, recorded at Isaiah 14:9, according to *The Amplified Old Testament* translation: "Sheol (Hades) below is stirred up to meet you at your coming [O tyrant Babylonian rulers]; it stirs up the shades of the dead to greet you, even all the chief ones of the earth; it raises from their thrones [in astonishment at your humbled condition] all the kings of the nations." The reader is urged to consider the entire context; it is a very interesting study.

Give consideration to the words recorded at Ezekiel 32:21, *A.S.V.*:

The strong among the mighty shall speak to him out of the midst of Sheol with them that help him; they are gone

176

down, they lie still, even the uncircumcised, slain by the sword.

The Amplified Old Testament renders this text thus:

The strong among the mighty shall speak of [Pharaoh] out of the midst of Sheol—the nether world— with those who helped him; they are gone down, they lie still, even the uncircumcised—the heathen—slain by the sword.

Here is how the *Moffatt* translation renders the text:

The mighty warriors in the underworld shall hail him and his allies: "Down with you, down, to a shameful death, you and all your host, amid victims of the sword!"

What have we learned thus far? That *Sheol* is down—way down—and that part of it is spoken of as "the lowest Sheol", a place to be dreaded. We also see that it is a place of conscious existence.

NEW TESTAMENT

At this point we shall consider Luke 16:19-31 from *The New English Bible*:

There was once a rich man, who dressed in purple and the finest linen, and feasted in great magnificence every day. At his gate, covered with sores, lay a poor man named Lazarus, who would have been glad to satisfy his hunger with the scraps from the rich man's table. Even the dogs used to come and lick his sores. One day the poor man died and was carried away by the angels to be with Abraham. The rich man also died and was buried, and in Hades, where he was in torment, he looked up; and there, far away was Abraham with Lazarus close beside him. "Abraham, my father," he called out, "take pity on me! Send Lazarus to dip the tip of his finger in water, to cool my tongue, for I am in agony in this fire."
But Abraham said, "Remember, my child, that all the

good things fell to you while you were alive, and all the bad to Lazarus; now he has his consolation here and it is you who are in agony. But that is not all: there is a great chasm fixed between us; no one from our side who wants to reach you can cross it, and none may pass from your side to us."

"Then, father," he replied, "will you send him to my father's house, where I have five brothers, to warn them, so they may not come to this place of torment?" Abraham said, "They have Moses and the prophets; let them listen to them." "No, father Abraham," he replied, "but if someone from the dead visits them, they will repent." Abraham answered, "If they do not listen to Moses and the prophets they will pay no heed even if someone should rise from the dead."

Luke 12:4, 5 (*A.S.V.*) reads as follows: "And I say unto you my friends. Be not afraid of them that kill the body, and after that have no more that they can do. But I will warn you whom ye shall fear: Fear him, who after he hath killed hath authority to cast into Gehenna" (see footnotes). Rotherham's translation reads: "And I say unto you my friends— Do not be put in fear of them who can kill the body, and after these things have nothing more uncommon which they can do. But I will suggest to you whom ye should fear—Fear him who after killing hath authority to cast into Gehenna."

Concerning the last judgment, we read at Revelation 20:11-15 (*New English Bible*):

Then I saw a great white throne, and the One who sat upon it; from his presence earth and heaven vanished away, and no place was left for them. I could see the dead, great and small, standing before the throne; and books were opened. Then another book was opened, the roll of the living. From what was written in these books the dead were judged upon the record of their deeds. The sea gave up its dead, and Death and Hades gave up the dead in their keeping; they were judged, each man on the record of his deeds. Then Death and Hades were flung into the lake of fire [Gehenna]. This lake of fire is the second death; and into it were flung any whose names were not to be found in the roll of the living.

Can one still believe what the Watch Tower Society teaches in view of what has already been said? Let us consider the subject yet further. Of Rachel's death Genesis 35:18 reads: "And it came to pass, as her SOUL WAS DEPARTING ..." (*A.S.V.*). Rotherham reads "when her soul was going forth". Even the *New World* translation reads "as her soul was going out". Furthermore, Elijah prayed over a dead child whose soul came into him again (1 Kings 17:21, 22).

But, says the Jehovah's Witness, what about Ezekiel 18:4, 20, where it says "the soul that sinneth, it shall die"? Reading the context, we find that the soul of a truly repentent person will *never* die! "Again, when the wicked man turneth away from his wickedness ... HE SHALL SAVE HIS SOUL ALIVE" (Ezekiel 18:27, *A.S.V.*).

We are reminded of Paul's words at 2 Corinthians 5:6, 8-10:

> Therefore we are always confident, knowing that, whilst we are at home in the body, we are absent from the Lord. We are confident, I say, and willing rather to be absent from the body, and to be present with the Lord. Wherefore we labour, that, whether present or absent, we may be accepted of him. For we must all appear before the judgment seat of Christ; that every one may receive the things done in his body, according to that he hath done, whether it be good or bad.

Reading this from *The Twentieth Century New Testament*:

> Therefore we are always confident, knowing that, while our home is in the body, we are absent from our home with the Lord. And in this confidence we would gladly leave our home in the body, and make our home with the Lord. Therefore, whether in our home or absent from our home, our one ambition is to please him. For at the Bar of the Christ we must all appear in our true characters, that each may reap the results of the life which he has lived in the body, in accordance with his actions—whether good or worthless.

If there is no spiritual soul within, then what is it that, in the case of a Christian, leaves the body and goes to be consciously present with the Lord? Do not try to say that this is the individual's "life record" (*The Watchtower*, April 15, 1963, page 241). For a record is neither conscious nor can it be rewarded.

"There is no man that hath power over the spirit to retain the spirit", says Ecclesiastes 8:8 (see *King James* and *Rotherham* translations). "For we know that—If our earthly tent-dwelling should be taken down, we have a building of God, a dwelling not made by hand, age-abiding in the heavens" (2 Corinthians 5:1, *Rotherham*). Reading this from *The Twentieth Century New Testament*: "For we know that if our tent—that earthly body which is now our home—is taken down, we have a house of God's building, a home not made by hands, imperishable, in Heaven."

What a wonderful promise!

THE BLESSED LIFE TO COME

"Don't let your heart be troubled. You believe in God, so believe also in Me. There are many rooms in My Father's house. Otherwise I would have told you. I am going to make ready a place for you. And when I have gone away and prepared a place, I shall come back to take you to Myself, so that you may be where I am. And where I am going, you know the Way ... I am the Way, the Truth and the Life. No one can come to the Father except through Me" (John 14: 1-4, 6, *The Simplified New Testament* by Olaf M. Norlie). "My beloved, we are God's children now, but exactly what we are to be hereafter has not yet been disclosed to us. But we know this, that when He appears we shall be like Him, for we shall see Him as He is" (1 John 3:2, Norlie). See also *The New Testament* by Charles B. Williams.

Yes, we shall see Him at His appearing. This truth is corroborated by Hebrews 9:27, 28: "And inasmuch as it is appointed for men to die once for all, and thereafter to be judged; So also shall Christ, offered once for all to bear the sins of many, be seen a second time for salvation apart from sin, by those who wait for him" (*The Historical New Testament*, Moffatt, 1901).

Not only shall believers see Him, they shall consciously abide with Him above. Of such blissful souls we read: " 'Who are these people clothed in the long white robes? And where have they come from?' 'My lord, you know,' I replied. 'They are those,' he said, 'who have just come out of the great distress, and have washed their robes and made them white in the blood of the Lamb. For this reason they stand before the very throne of God, and render Him service day and night in His sanctuary, and He who is sitting upon the throne will shelter them in his tent. Nevermore shall they hunger, nevermore shall they thirst, nevermore shall the sun smite them nor any scorching heat. For the Lamb who is before the throne will be their Shepherd, and will guide them to the water-springs of Life, and God will wipe every tear from their eyes.' " (Revelation 7:13-17, *Weymouth*). Notice, please, that this occurs *before* the first resurrection (Revelation 20), the resurrection of their bodies.

In spite of all this Scriptural evidence of the reality of a continuing life after death, *The Watchtower* magazine of April 15, 1963 makes mockery, ridicule, and scorn of the idea of an immaterial human soul and of any true resurrection of the body. Lest this article should persuade any who do not know the Bible well, we will give space to answering it.

RESURRECTION OF WHAT?

On page 231 the magazine asks this question:

... if the human soul cannot die but lives on in an invisible realm, how are there any dead to be raised and why is there need of a resurrection?

We reply: According to their theory, there is nothing to be resurrected, either in our case or in the case of Christ. (They believe He was obliterated, or annihilated.) But God Himself cannot resurrect *something* from *nothing*! Jehovah's Witnesses expect thin air to be resurrected! But wait—the J. W. will now say, "The dead remain in the memory of God; so, a memory remains." Well, then, how can you resurrect a memory? We still say that if there is nothing left of the individual who died, then God has nothing there to resurrect. Re-create, maybe—but not "resurrect". Consider the contents of a perfect vacuum. Could God resurrect *that*? According to the Watch Tower theory He could! They believe that there needs be nothing to be resurrected yet a resurrection can occur!

Also on page 231 they get involved with the Hebrew word *nefesh*. They indicate that *nefesh* is the person himself. This is what Genesis 2:7 indicates. God breathed into man the *neshamah* of life, and man became a *nefesh chaiah*—"living being" (Moffatt). Or, as the magazine states, a "person". And so we could rightly translate the words of Genesis 2:7 "man became a living person". Here they have said nothing new, but have stated a truth which previously they have not acknowledged.

On page 233 this issue of *The Watchtower* magazine grinds its old axe regarding Ezekiel 18:4, 20—"the soul that sinneth, it shall die". This was answered earlier in this chapter so we shall not repeat that answer here. Further on this page they point out Matthew 10:28—"fear him who is able to DESTROY both soul and body in hell". They think this teaches annihilation of the soul. The Greek word translated *destroy* is *apollumi*, and appears also in verse 6, there translated *lost*. At Romans 14:15 the *New World* Bible (Watchtower) translates this word *ruin*. At 1 Corinthians 1:19 they render it *perish*. At 2 Corinthians 4:3 *perishing*. John 6:12 *wasted*. Not only at Matthew 10:6 and 15:24 do they translate it *lost*, but also at Luke 15:4, 6, 9, 24, 32; 19:10; John 18:9. In the following texts they translate it *lose*: Matthew 10:39, 42; 16:25; Mark 8:35; 9:41; Luke 9:24, 25; 15:8; 17:33; John 6:39, 2 John 8. So they themselves acknowledge this word *apollumi* carries meanings other than "destroy".

So we conclude therefrom that at Matthew 10:28 (in view of what so many other Scriptures say regarding the soul) the word *apollumi* is used in the sense that the soul in *gehenna* is *lost* (eternally), and hence has *perished*, though still consciously existent.

On page 236 this magazine quotes Acts 1:9-11. Note these words: "Ye men of Galilee, why stand ye gazing into heaven? this SAME JESUS, which is taken up from you into heaven, SHALL SO COME IN LIKE MANNER AS YE HAVE SEEN HIM GO into heaven." Did they see Him or did they not? If they saw Him ascend, He will be seen when He descends. In contradiction to this, note these words from page 237 of *The Watchtower* magazine quoted previously:

If Jesus were to take his body of flesh, blood and bones to heaven and enjoy them there, what would this mean? It would mean that there would be no resurrection of the dead for anybody. Why not? Because Jesus would be taking his sacrifice off God's altar.

We fail to get the point here. The Watch Tower teaches that not only was the sacrifice taken off the altar (the cross) but that it (flesh, bones *and* blood) was annihilated. They believe that once the body was entombed God got rid of it.

The body was not supposed to remain on the altar nor in the tomb very long (Psalms 16:10; Acts 2:27; 13:35). So the question is not whether or not the body was taken off the altar, but what happened to it afterwards. Did it see corruption (decay, disintegration) or did it not?

Reading further on this same page we come across these words:

(John 6:51, 54, 55) How could we eat Jesus' flesh and drink his blood in order to have everlasting life and at the same time Jesus himself have the flesh and blood themselves in which to live in heaven? It is a common proverb that a person cannot have his cake and eat it too.

To which we reply: Jesus offered the cup and wafer to his apostles, saying:

Then He took a loaf [of bread], and when He had given thanks He broke [it] and gave it to them saying, This is My body which is given for you. Do this in remembrance of Me. And in like manner He took the cup after supper, saying, This cup is the new testament *or* covenant [ratified] in My blood which is shed (poured out) for you. (Luke 22:19, 20 *Amplified New Testament*).

How could He offer blood that had not yet been shed? How could He offer a body not yet sacrificed? It was the same situation then as now (holding to the bodily resurrection teaching).

The next paragraph goes on to say:

Since clergymen who insist that Jesus has his human body

183

in heaven teach that he is also God himself, then we know what God looks like.

That would be so IF the individual believed in Sabellianism, that is, that Christ is all of God, and God exists in one Person only. However, by far the majority of those believing in the deity of Christ are *trinitarians*, NOT Sabellians! The writer is himself a trinitarian and so understands the position of the trinitarians.

WHAT KIND OF A BODY?

On page 240 this *Watchtower* magazine says, regarding Christ:

If Jesus had been resurrected human, he would again have borne the image of the "first man Adam". Hence in becoming like Jesus in their resurrection his followers would be bearing again the "image of the one made of dust" and not the image of anyone heavenly.

To which we reply from 1 John 3:2 according to *The Amplified New Testament*:

Beloved, we are [even here] now God's children; it is not yet disclosed (made clear) what we shall be [hereafter], but we know that when He comes *and* is manifested we shall [as God's children] resemble *and* be like Him, for WE SHALL SEE HIM just as He [really] is.

God will not create entirely new entities, pure spirit forms without any relation to our present physical bodies, but will raise up and redo the very body that was deposited in the earth. This can be inferred from the term "resurrection", is clearly stated in Romans 8:11 and 1 Corinthians 15:53, and is implied in the figure of the seed sown in the earth which Paul employs in 1 Corinthians 15:35-38. However, they shall definitely be changed—not unresurrected bodies like Adam's. But *bodies* they shall be, redone by God. Not that the mortal bodies will be raised (Romans 8:11), and then fitted for new life in heaven.

Let us stray from our basis subject for a moment in order to analyze two interesting statements in this issue. One from page 240:

What about the billions of people, including faithful men and women of God, who died without a heavenly hope prior to Christ's first coming? And what about people today? Hundreds of thousands of godly men and women are living without a heavenly hope.

By "people today" they are referring to the Witnesses baptized after 1931, who cannot go to heaven. They continue on page 241:

So it will be with persons who remain part of the earthly seed of mankind and who have not been begotten of God's spirit ...

Notice in particular that last sentence—"who have not been begotten of God's spirit"! Let us read Romans 8:9 with regard to this situation:

You are on the spiritual level, if only God's Spirit dwells within you; AND IF A MAN DOES NOT POSSESS THE SPIRIT OF CHRIST, HE IS NO CHRISTIAN (*New English Bible*). See also the *New World Translation*.

Reading now Romans 8:11 according to *The Twentieth Century New Testament*:

If the Spirit of him who raised Jesus from the dead lives within you, he who raised Christ Jesus from the dead will give Life even to your mortal bodies, through his Spirit living within you.

Then read Romans 8:14 from any translation of the Bible you choose. The King James Bible states: "FOR AS MANY AS ARE LED BY THE SPIRIT OF GOD, THEY ARE THE SONS OF GOD."

So hundreds of thousands of Jehovah's Witnesses are neither Christians nor sons of God, for they do not belong to

Him. Nor can they experience any supernatural life or the leading of the Holy Spirit. What a pitiful condition! We shall take up this subject again in the next chapter.

DENIAL OF LITERAL RESURRECTION

Jehovah's Witnesses evidently realize that their teaching actually denies resurrection in the true sense of the word. Of the four meanings given the word in the Thorndike-Barnhart dictionary, the fourth is: "Restoration from decay, disuse, etc.; revival." Since Jehovah's Witnesses teach there is nothing left to be restored or revived, rather than teach a true resurrection they teach recreation. And so they state on page 241 of the above-quoted *Watchtower* magazine: "These inspired words [Psalm 104:29, 30] assure us that Almighty God can re-create, yes, re-create human souls." In lieu of a proper resurrection they teach a re-creation.

SUMMING UP

On page 247 of this issue of *The Watchtower* states:

Christians show appreciation for the miracle of Christ's resurrection, not by celebrating a certain day set aside by some ancient council of men, and doing so with pagan appendages, but by accepting by faith the fact of Jesus' resurrection and by letting it give them hope for their dead loved ones and themselves ...

We note, however, that the hope of Jehovah's Witnesses is to keep going out and selling books and magazines; keep going to the Kingdom Hall for four meetings a week; keep going to the area group studies every week; keep going to the conventions every year, etc. In order to gain salvation! Personal faith in Christ's finished work is not enough. But what has Christ's sacrifice to do with all this? Could one not work for his salvation apart from Christ, the way Jehovah's Witnesses accept Him? Of course!

Now if we preach that Christ has been raised from the dead, how is it that some of you are saying that there is no such thing as a resurrection of the dead? If there is no resurrection of the dead, then Christ has not been raised, and if Christ was not raised, the message which we preach has nothing in it; there is nothing in our faith either, and we are found guilty of lying about God, for we have testified that He raised Christ, whom He did not raise, if indeed the dead are never raised.

For if the dead are not raised, Christ has not been raised; and if Christ has not been raised, your faith is a mere delusion; you are still under the penalty of your sins. Yes, even those who have fallen asleep, though in no union with Christ, have perished. If for this life only we Christians have set our hopes on Christ, we are the most pitiable people in the world. (1 Corinthians 15:12-18, *The New Testament* by Charles B. Williams).

And so I believe in the continuance of life hereafter, because it is taught in Scripture. For the same reason I believe in the resurrection of the body and its glorification like unto Christ's body.

13

How Can A Man Be Born Again?

VIEWPOINT OF THE WATCHTOWER

Quoting *The Watchtower* magazine of November 15, 1954 on the subject: "Who Are Born Again" we read as follows:

Christ introduced the subject of being "born again". It is a subject that, down through the centuries, has been little understood. Many religious leaders today hold to the view that if one is not "born again" there is no salvation. In other words, being "born again", they say, is the only way to salvation.

To understand what it means to be "born again" one must know who are "born again". Note carefully that, in discussing this matter, Jesus did not say that all who gain everlasting life must be "born again". Rather, what he said was that unless one was "born again" he could not see the "kingdom of God".

Now the kingdom of God is heavenly. Jehovah has purposed that the Kingdom be the capital or ruling part of his universal organization. Jehovah also purposed that a limited number, taken from among mankind, would reign with Christ Jesus as associate kings. For this sublime privilege they must be resurrected and given spirit bodies, since, as the apostle said, "flesh and blood cannot inherit God's kingdom".

That the Father has set a limitation on the number of those who will reign with his Son in the heavenly kingdom is manifest from Jesus' words: "Have no fear, little flock, because your Father has approved of giving you the kingdom." The exact number of the "little flock" approved by the Father to be Kingdom heirs was not known until Christ, through an angel, revealed it to be 144,000 "who have been purchased from the earth". This "little flock" of 144,000 Kingdom heirs, then, are those ones from among mankind who are "born again".

Jesus was the first one to be "born again".

Yet they teach that Jesus is NOT one of the 144,000! Note also: Jesus Himself needed the new birth! Little wonder they do not worship *him*! But the Bible teaches that Jesus is our Redeemer, Jehovah the Son. Here let us read Job 19:25, 26 according to the Rotherham translation (see footnotes):

> But I know that my redeemer liveth, and later on over my dust will he arise; and though after my skin is struck off this bundle of bones, yet apart from my flesh shall I see God.

Isaiah said the redeemer was Jehovah; reading Isaiah 47:4 (*A.S.V.*): "Our Redeemer, Jehovah of hosts is his name, the Only One of Israel."

SAVED FROM WHAT TO WHAT?

We can only explain a subject such as this by starting at the very beginning, showing what we need to be redeemed *from*; then, when such redemption has come, showing what the one so redeemed has been redeemed *to*.

The transgression in Eden called for a sentence of death. Man had fallen from his true sonship with God. God was no longer man's Father and man was no longer God's son. The sentence of death was passed, yet man continued to live (physically). But he lived in *spiritual* death. His life radically changed. The change was for the worse.

God designed to save man from his fallen condition and restore him to sonship again. Of course, a requirement was attached, just as man was originally given a requirement if he hoped to keep his sonship as it was. This requirement was that God and man must be reunited by man's acceptance of the means He would provide.

Since the death sentence concerned more than just man's body (for he was spiritually dead while yet physically alive), his receiving new life would also concern more than just his body. Whatever had died, *that* must live again. How? Well,

189

life originates from birth, does it not? Therefore where life has not previously existed but does now exist, we say there has been a *birth*.

Yet this birth (in the case of fallen man), would not apply to his being born into this world (physically). Why so? Because the children of fallen man would be permitted to be born dead (spiritually). They would be physically alive as was Adam, when he was dead in the sight of God. This would pass on to future generations, which would all be born spiritually dead. God designed to accept sacrifices on behalf of spiritually dead persons, that would atone for them. These sacrifices involved blood.

The first of such sacrifices was given by Abel, who gave "the firstlings of his flock" (Genesis 4:4). Jesus was the final sacrifice and the complete one. Before Jesus gave Himself to die, He told one that he "must be born again" (John 3:3). This new birth was prior to the sacrifices of the Son of God. You see, all believers who acted upon God's provision for atonement in faith, through the typical sacrifices ordained by God, looked *forward* to the sacrifice of Messiah, as today we look *backward* to it, in faith. The new birth did not originate with Jesus Christ, but had been God's provision from the very start to thus reunite believing mankind with the heavenly Father.

How far reaching would this new birth become? To what position did it restore us? It would be impossible to be restored to Adam's original position again, for we are now in bodies of sin and the new birth is only given to us spiritually (it does not make our physical bodies perfect until the rapture of the Church). We will not become carbon copies of Adam before the fall. The sin nature caused spiritual death. We are to be considered "crucified with Christ". As such we would be considered sons of God. So you see the position we are in (after our new birth) does not correspond to that position of Adam before the fall.

A person can be born again only by being redeemed (saved) FROM the sentence of death placed upon Adam's posterity, TO the likeness of the Son of God Himself!

RESURRECTION OF JESUS CHRIST INVOLVED

The reason Jehovah's Witnesses have strayed so far from

the truth of this matter is because they refuse to recognize the bodily resurrection of Jesus Christ. With no Scriptural authority whatsoever, they blindly assume that Jesus' body was destroyed in some manner not disclosed in the Bible, and that He was re-created as a spirit.

They declare that His appearances following His "resurrection" were materializations. We might note these words of Christ, recorded at Luke 24:39, 40:

> Behold my hands and my feet, that it is I myself; handle me, and see; for a spirit hath not flesh and bones, as ye see me have. And when he had thus spoken, he showed them his hands and his feet.

Reading the account of the resurrection as given in John 20:3-7:

> Peter therefore went forth, and the other disciple, and they went toward the tomb. And they ran both together: and the other disciple outran Peter, and came first to the tomb; and stooping down and looking in, he seeth the linen clothes lying; yet entered he not in. Simon Peter therefore also cometh, following him, and entered into the tomb; and he beholdeth the linen clothes lying, and the napkin, that was upon his head, not lying with the linen clothes, but rolled up in a place by itself.

The tomb had been sealed, a watch had been placed, and the stone not rolled away with human hands. Question: Who was inside that tomb to thus arrange the burial garments of the swaddled body? IF that body had been disposed of in some manner, why not the burial garments with it? Why were they still there? They held no special significance, according to Jehovah's Witnesses! Who put them where they were? And why was the body removed? If Christ was re-created as a spirit, what difference would it have made whether or not his fleshly body was still there? Why did the angel beckon the onlookers to go see for themselves that *he*, the literal, physical body of Jesus, was *not* there? If His body had still been there, would that have proven that He had not been raised? No! answers the Jehovah's Witness! So, from their point of view, all these facts and events were purposeless.

191

Just exactly how does the resurrection of Christ come into the subject of the new birth? In this way: He was raised in a physical body later glorified upon His ascension. We, too, are to be raised with like glorified, physical bodies. (IF we have been born again!) We read of this at Philippians 3:20, 21 according to *The Twentieth Century New Testament* translation:

But the State of which we are citizens is in Heaven; and it is from Heaven that we are eagerly looking for a Saviour, the Lord Jesus Christ, who, by the exercise of his power to bring everything into subjection to himself, will make this body that we have in our humiliation like to that body which he has in his Glory.

So the new birth not only redeems us while we are here, but raises us to heaven itself. The soul rests in the presence of the Lord until the resurrection (Revelation 6:9-11).

Jehovah's Witnesses believe that before Christ's sacrifice all God's people were of the "earthly class". They believe that when Christ revealed that there would be a "heavenly class" He was speaking of the 144,000, named in the book of Revelation, chapters seven and fourteen. Therefore, they hold that the new birth (such as they accept it) is only for those composing the 144,000.

There are two classes of people in the Bible, all right, but they are the saved and the lost; or, the righteous and the wicked. The Psalms state: "Let the wicked be put to shame, let them be silent in Sheol" (31:17, *A.S.V.*). Then consider the words from Psalm 32:5-7 (*A.S.V.*):

I acknowledged my sin unto thee, and mine iniquity did I not hide: I said, I will confess my transgressions unto Jehovah; and thou forgavest the iniquity of my sin. For this let every one that is godly pray unto thee in the time of finding out sin; surely when the waters overflow they shall not reach unto him. Thou art my hiding-place; thou wilt preserve me from trouble; thou wilt compass me about with songs of deliverance.

Paul did not divide the believers into two classes, but said (2 Timothy, 4:8, *A.S.V.*):

Henceforth there is laid up for me the crown of righteousness, which the Lord, the righteous judge, shall give me at that day; and not to me only, but also TO ALL THEM THAT HAVE LOVED HIS APPEARING.

How inclusive was Jesus in His invitation to believers? "All that the Father giveth me SHALL come to me; and him that cometh to me I will in no wise cast out" (John 6:37). "This is my Father's will, that every one who holds to the Son of God and believes in Him should have eternal life, and I will raise him to life on the last day" (John 6:40, Weymouth). "I am the living bread which came down out of heaven: if ANY MAN eat of this bread, he shall live forever" (John 6:51, A.S.V.).

If and when you *do* come to Christ, it will be because the Father has drawn you; not that you suddenly decided that you would like to come to Christ at some time convenient to yourself. "No man can come *to* me, except the Father which hath sent me draw him: and I will raise him up at the last day" (John 6:44). "Therefore said I unto you, that no man can come unto me except it were given unto him of my Father. From that time many of his disciples went back, and walked no more with him" (John 6:65, 66).

ATONEMENT FOR ETERNITY

Let us read about Messiah and determine what purpose lay behind His coming. We read the following from the fifty-third chapter of Isaiah, verses 2-9, quoting *The Amplified Old Testament* translation:

For the servant of God grew up before Him like a tender plant, and as a root out of dry ground; He has no beautiful form or comeliness that we should look at Him, and no beauty that we should desire Him. He was despised and rejected *and* forsaken by men, a Man of sorrows *and* pains, and acquainted with grief *and* sickness; and as one from Whom men hide their faces He was despised, and we did not appreciate His worth *or* have any esteem for Him.

Surely He has borne our griefs—sickness, weakness and distress—and carried our sorrows *and* pain [of punishment]. Yet we ignorantly considered Him stricken, smitten and afflicted by God (as if with leprosy). [Matt. 8:17].

But He was wounded for our transgressions, He was bruised for our guilt *and* iniquities; the chastisement needful to obtain peace *and* well-being for us was upon Him, and with stripes that wounded Him we are healed *and* made whole.

All we like sheep have gone astray, we have turned every one to his own way; and the Lord has made to light on Him the guilt *and* iniquity of us all. [1 Pet. 2:24, 25.] He was oppressed, yet when He was afflicted He was submissive *and* opened not His mouth; as a lamb that is led to the slaughter, and as a sheep that before her shearers is dumb, so He opened not His mouth.

By oppression and judgment He was taken away; and as for His generation, who among them considered that He was cut off out of the land of the living for the transgression of my [Isaiah's] people, to whom the stroke was due —stricken to His death? And they assigned Him a grave with the wicked and with a rich man in His death, although He had done no violence, neither was any deceit in His mouth. [Matt. 27:57-60; 1 Pet. 2:22, 23.]

Yet even more startling is Paul's statement that Christ was made sin for us: "Him who knew no sin WAS MADE TO BE SIN ON OUR BEHALF; that we might become the righteousness of God in him" (2 Corinthians 5:21, *A.S.V.*). Your sins and mine were nailed to that cross. Speaking of Christ's last moments on the cross, John R. W. Stott in his book *Basic Christianity* (William B. Eerdmans Publishing Co., $1.25) says on page 96:

At once, emerging from that outer darkness, He cried in triumph, "It is finished", and then, "Father, into thy hands I commit my spirit", and He died (Jn. xix. 30; Lk. xxiii. 46). The work He had come to do was finished. The salvation He had come to win was accomplished. The sins of the world were borne. Reconciliation to God was available to all who would trust this Saviour for themselves, and receive Him as their own.

So, as if to give a public witness to this fact, the unseen hand of God tore down the veil of the Temple and hurled it aside. It was needed no longer. The way into God's holy presence was no longer barred. Christ had "opened the gate of heaven to all believers"

Paul speaks regarding our entrance into the benefits provided by Christ's death at Romans 6:2-8, Weymouth's translation:

How can we who have died to sin, live in it any longer? Or do you not know that all of us who were baptized into Christ Jesus were baptized into His death? Well, then, by our baptism we were buried with Him in death, in order that, just as Christ was raised from the dead by the Father's glorious power, we also should live an entirely new life. For if we have become one with Him by sharing in His death, we shall also be one with Him by sharing in His resurrection. This we know—that our old self was nailed to the cross with Him, in order that our sinful nature might be neutralized, so that we should no longer be the slaves of sin; for he who has died is absolved from his sin. But if we have died with Christ, we believe that we shall also live with Him.

A person is born again by the miracle of new birth being performed through an act beginning with repentance and faith. His growth as a result of his new birth is governed by the indwelling Holy Spirit.

CONFESSION OF CHRIST BRINGS NEW BIRTH

"If with your mouth you confess Jesus as Lord and in your heart you believe that God raised Him from the dead, you shall be saved" (Romans 10:9, Weymouth). These new-born ones are not *slaves* but are *friends* of God: "I call you servants no longer; a servant does not know what his master is about. I have called you friends, because I have disclosed to you everything that I heard from my Father" (John 15:15, *New English Bible*).

"Surely you know that you are God's temple, where the Spirit of God dwells" (1 Corinthians 3·16, *New English Bible*). "Guard the treasure put into our charge, with the help of the Holy Spirit dwelling within us" (1 Timothy 1:14, *New English Bible*).

THE PASSING FROM DEATH UNTO LIFE

You are either dead or alive, spiritually—not *both*. The

Scriptures on this matter are many and they are plain. Many things hinder you from accepting them, but they are there nonetheless. Consider first the words of 2 Thessalonians 2: 13-15, quoting the Weymouth translation:

But from us thanks are always due to God on your behalf, brethren whom the Lord loves, because God from the beginning has chosen you for salvation through the Spirit's sanctifying influence and your belief in the truth. To this He has called you by our gospel, so that you may attain to the glory of our Lord Jesus Christ. So then, brethren stand firm, and hold fast to the teachings which you have received from us, whether by word of mouth or by letter.

Yes, the fact that *God* has chosen us is what makes the change permanent. The Lord further assures us of our salvation is these words from Isaiah 51:4-6, according to *The Amplified Old Testament* translation:

Listen to Me, the Lord, O My people, and give ear to Me, O My nation; for a [divine gospel] law will go forth from Me and I will establish My justice for a light to the peoples. My rightness *and* justice are near, My salvation is gone forth, and My arms shall rule the peoples; the islands shall wait for *and* expect Me, and on My arm shall they trust *and* wait with hope.

Lift up your eyes to the heavens, and look upon the earth beneath; for the heavens shall be dissolved *and* vanish away like smoke, and the earth shall wax old like a garment, and they that dwell therein shall die in like manner—like gnats; but My salvation shall be for ever, and My rightness *and* justice [and faithfully fulfilled promise] shall not be abolished. [Matt. 24:35; 2 Pet. 3:10; Heb. 1:11.]

The born-again ones are seen by John and described in Revelation 7:9-12, Moffatt:

After that I looked, and there was a great host whom no one could count, from every nation and tribe and people and tongue, standing before the throne and before the Lamb, clad in white robes, with palm-branches in their hands; and they cried with a loud voice, "Saved by our God who is seated on the throne, and by the Lamb!"

And all the angels surrounded the throne and the Presbyters and the four living Creatures, and fell on their faces before the throne, worshipping God and crying, "Even so! Blessing and glory and wisdom and thanksgiving and honour and power and might be to our God for ever and ever: Amen!"

The essence of the transformation from death to life is contained in John 5:24, quoted from *The Twentieth Century New Testament*:

In truth I tell you that he who listens to my Message and believes him who sent me, has Immortal Life, and does not come under condemnation, but has already passed out of Death into Life.

Paul echoes this thought at Romans 8:1, 2, using the same translation as above:

There is, therefore, now no condemnation for those who are in union with Christ Jesus; for through your union with Christ Jesus, the Law of the life-giving Spirit has set you free from the Law of Sin and Death [mentioned in Romans 6:23].

The miraculous transformation takes place the instant we accept Christ; the believer then possesses (from that moment on) eternal life. Reading 1 John 5:10-13 from the translation by H. B. Montgomery:

He who believes on the Son of God has the testimony in himself. He who does not believe God, has made him a liar, because he has not believed in the testimony that God has borne concerning his Son. And the testimony is this, "God has given us eternal life, and this life is in his Son" He who has the Son has life; he who has not the Son of God has not the life. I have written these words to you so that you may know that you have eternal life, you who believe in the name of the Son of God.

Note these words from Acts 13:48, using Weymouth's translation:

The Gentiles listened with delight and extolled the Lord's word; and all who were predestined to eternal life believed.

Reading now Hebrews 9:12 from Moffatt's 1922 translation:

Not taking any blood of goats and oxen but his own blood, and so entered once and for all into the Holy place, securing a redemption that is eternal.

Isaiah describes that blessed time to come. Quoting chapter 33:20-24, Moffatt:

You shall see your quiet home, Jerusalem immovable, a tent whose pegs shall never be pulled up, whose ropes are never to be rent. And there, instead of broad streams circling round, we have the glorious Eternal as our river, a river never raided by a galley, sailed by no ships of war.
The Eternal himself rules us, the Eternal is our captain, the Eternal is our king, he, he alone, defends us; even blind folk shall share rich plunder, even lame folk loot at large; none in the land shall say then: "I am sick", for all who live there have their sins forgiven.

SINS UNDER THE BLOOD

"The blood of Jesus his Son cleanseth us from all sin" (1 John 1:7, *A.S.V.*). Romans 5:9 tells us we are "justified by his blood". From Hebrews 9:22 (*A.S.V.*): "According to the law, I may say, all things are cleansed with blood, AND APART FROM SHEDDING OF BLOOD THERE IS NO REMISSION." 1 Peter 1:18, 19 reminds us: "Forasmuch as ye know that ye were not redeemed with corruptible things ... but with the PRECIOUS BLOOD OF CHRIST." Give mind to the words recorded at Acts 20:28 (*Twentieth Century New Testament*): "Be watchful over yourselves, and over the whole flock, of which the Holy Spirit has placed you in charge, to shepherd the Church of God, which he acquired through HIS OWN BLOOD."
Give thought also to the words of Ephesians 1:5-7, Weymouth's translation:

For he predestined us to be adopted by Himself as sons through Jesus Christ—such being His precious will and pleasure—to the praise of the splendour of His grace with which He has enriched us in the beloved One. It is in Him, and THROUGH THE SHEDDING OF HIS BLOOD, that we have our deliverance.

CHRIST IN YOU; YOU IN CHRIST

"Dwell in Me and I will dwell in you.—Live in Me and I will live in you. If a person does not dwell in Me, he is thrown out as a branch and withers. Such branches are gathered up and thrown into the fire and they are burned" (John 15:4, 6 *Amplified New Testament*). "They will put you out of the synagogues [also the Kingdom Halls!]—expel you. But an hour is coming when whoever kills you will think *and* claim that he has offered service to God. And they will do this because they have not known the Father nor Me" (John 16:2, 3 *Amplified New Testament*).

If you are with Him now you are going to be with Him forever and ever:

Father, I desire that these men, who are thy gift to me, may be with me where I am, so that they may look upon my glory, which thou hast given me because thou didst love me before the world began (John 17:24, *New English Bible*).

Reading Ephesians 1:3, 4, using Charles B. Williams translation:

Blessed be the God and Father of our Lord Jesus Christ, who through Christ has blessed us with every spiritual blessing in the heavenly realm. Through Him He picked us out before the creation of the world, to be consecrated and above reproach in His sight in love.

Such ones had their names recorded in the book of life from the foundation of the world—see Revelation 17:8. Of them 1 Peter 1:2 (Moffatt, 1922) states: "Whom God the Father has predestined and chosen, by the consecration of the Spirit, to obey Jesus Christ and be sprinkled with his blood."

199

TURN TO ME AND YOU ARE SAVED!

These words are expressed at Isaiah 45:22, again using Moffatt's translation: "Turn to me and you are saved, all ends of the earth! As I am God and God alone, I swear by myself, I swear a true word, never to be recalled, that every knee shall bow to me, and every tongue swear loyalty."

Have you ever felt like David when he said, "O that I had wings like a dove! I would fly away and be at rest" (Psalm 55:6, *Amplified Old Testament*). Then "come unto me, all ye that labour and are heavy laden, and I will give you rest" (Matthew 11:28). Turn to Christ now and be saved.

HOW FIRM A FOUNDATION?

Is salvation a shaky understanding that can be had now and lost a moment later? Jehovah's Witnesses say so. Exactly how firm *is* the foundation upon which we rest? Consider here the words of John R. W. Stott in his book *Basic Christianity* under the subject "A Secure Relationship", beginning on page 137:

> Supposing we have entered this intimate relationship with God, and are assured of it by God's own word, is it a secure relationship? Or can we be born into God's family one moment and repudiated from it the next? The Bible indicates it is a permanent relationship. "If children, then heirs," wrote St. Paul, "heirs of God and fellow heirs with Christ" (Rom. viii. 17).
> "But what happens if and when I sin?" you may ask. "Do I not then forfeit my sonship and cease to be God's child?" No. Think of the analogy of a human family. A young man is rude to his parents. A cloud descends on the home. There is tension in the atmosphere. Father and son are not on speaking terms. What has happened? Has the boy ceased to be a son?
> No. Their relationship has not changed; it is their fellowship which has been spoiled. Relationship depends on birth; fellowship depends on behaviour. As soon as the young man apologizes, he is forgiven. And forgiveness restores fellowship. Meanwhile, his relationship has remained the same. He may have been temporarily a disobedient, and even a defiant son; but he has not ceased to be a son.

So it is with the children of God. When we sin, we do not forfeit our relationship to Him as children, though our fellowship with Him is marred until we confess our sin. As soon as we "confess our sins, he is faithful and just, and will forgive our sins and cleanse us from all unrighteousness," for "if any one does sin, we have an advocate with the Father, Jesus Christ the righteous; and he is the expiation for our sins" (Jn. i. 9, ii. 1, 2).

So when you fall, fall on your knees and humbly seek your Father's forgiveness at once. Keep short accounts with Him. Aim to preserve your conscience clear and undefiled.

THE GREAT TEXT

To sum up we need only quote the most familiar text in the New Testament, John 3:16:

For God so loved the world, that he gave his only begotten Son, that whosoever believeth in him should not perish, but have everlasting life.

Do you believe it?—and Him? Confess it! I did, and a marvellous thing happened to me. I was born again.

Let us go further, speaking on this passing over from eternal night to eternal day.

14

Born Of The Spirit By The Dying Lamb

BIRTH IN DEATH

"And I saw in the midst of the throne and the four living creatures and in the midst of the elders a Lamb standing, showing that it had been slain" (Revelation 5:6, Rotherham). "Then I noticed a Lamb standing in the midst of the throne and the four living Creatures and the Presbyters; it seemed to have been slain" (Moffatt). "Then I saw standing in the very middle of the throne, inside the circle of living creatures and the circle of the elders, a Lamb with the marks of slaughter upon him" (*New English Bible*). "Then, within the space between the throne and the four Creatures, and in the midst of the Councillors, I saw, standing, a Lamb, which seemed to have been sacrificed" (*Twentieth Century New Testament*).

"That which is born of the flesh is flesh; and that which is BORN OF THE SPIRIT is spirit. Marvel not that I said unto thee Ye must be born again" (John 3:6, 7). "The Spirit breathes where it will, and thou hearest its voice, but thou knowest not whence it comes, or where it goes; thus it is with every one who has been BORN OF THE SPIRIT" (John 3:8, *The Emphatic Diaglott*). "The Spirit breatheth where it will, and thou hearest the voice thereof, but knowest not whence it cometh, and whither it goeth: so is every one that is BORN OF THE SPIRIT" (*A.S.V.*, see footnote).

The new birth comes from, through, or by means of Christ, the Lamb of God. The account in the third chapter of John goes on to relate the following:

And just as Moses in the desert lifted up the serpent on the pole, the Son of Man must be lifted up [on the cross, footnote], so that everyone who trusts in Him may have eternal life.

Whoever trusts in Him is never to come up for judgment; but whosoever does not trust in Him has already received his sentence, because he has not trusted in the name of God's only Son.

The above texts are from John 3:14, 15, 18, *Twentieth Century New Testament*. Verse 36 states: "Whoever trusts in the Son possesses eternal life, but whoever refuses to trust in the Son will not see life, but the wrath of God continues to remain on him."

You see, the believer has been born into life eternal, through Jesus Christ. The blood of the Lamb cancels out the death-dealing sin:

No distinction is made; for all alike have sinned, and consciously fall short of the glory of God, but are acquitted freely by His grace through the ransom given in Christ Jesus, whom God put forward as a propitiation available to faith IN VIRTUE OF HIS BLOOD (Romans 3:23, 24, Weymouth).

The wages of Sin are Death, but the gift of God is Immortal Life, through union with Christ Jesus, our Lord (Romans 6:23, *Twentieth Century New Testament*).

So that, just as when sin reigned, death was the result, so also when grace reigns, everlasting life is the result through justification by Jesus Christ, our Lord (Romans 5:21, Norlie).

Our spiritual birth happens now as a result of personal faith in the death of our Lord, the Lamb of God. By His death we have new birth—spiritually. My new birth occurred when I saw in the dying Lamb the love of God toward my soul.

This blessed Lamb of God was "slain from the foundation of the world" (Revelation 13:8). Slain so we may become born of the Spirit. The thief on the cross was born of the Spirit by the dying Lamb:

One of the criminals who were hanging beside Jesus railed at him. "Are you not the Christ? Save yourself and us," he said. But the other rebuked him. "Have not you," he said, "any fear of God, now that you are under the same sentence? And we justly so, for we are wrong. Jesus," he went on, "do not forget me when you have come to your kingdom." And Jesus answered: "I tell you, this very day you shall be with me in Paradise" (Luke 23:39-42, *Twentieth Century New Testament*).

Because the Watch Tower Society denies that the thief was saved at that very instant, we quote the following from *Matthew Henry's Commentary* (One Volume), page 1498:

This malefactor was snatched as a brand out of the burning, and made a monument of divine mercy and grace. This is no encouragement to any to put off their repentance, for, though it is certain that true repentance is never too late, it is as certain that late repentance is seldom true. He never had any offer of Christ, nor day of grace, before now; he was designed to be made a singular instance of the power of Christ's grace. Christ, having conquered Satan in the description of Judas and the preservation of Peter, erects this further trophy of his victory over him. We shall see the case to be extraordinary if we observe,

[1] The extraordinary operations of God's grace upon him, which appeared in what he said. *First,* See what he said to the other malefactor, v. 40, 41. 1. He reproved him for railing at Christ, as destitute of the *fear of God*: *Dost thou not fear God*? This implies that it was the fear of God which restrained him from following the multitude to do this evil. "If thou hadst any humanity in thee, thou wouldest not insult over one that is thy fellow-sufferer; *thou art in the same condition*; thou art a *dying man* too."

2. He owns that he deserves what was done to him: *We indeed justly. We received the due reward of our deeds.* True penitents acknowledge the justice of God is all the punishments of their sin. God has *done right*, but *we have done wickedly*.

3. He believes Christ to have suffered *wrongfully*. This penitent thief is convinced, by his conduct in his sufferings, that *he has done nothing amiss*. The chief priests would have him *crucified between* the malefactors, as *one of them*; but this thief has more sense then they.

Secondly, See what he said to our Lord Jesus: Lord, *remember me when thou comest into thy kingdom,* v. 42. This is the prayer of a *dying sinner* to a *dying Saviour.* It was the honour of Christ to be *thus prayed to.* It was the happiness of the thief *thus to pray;* perhaps he never prayed before, and yet now was heard, and saved at the last gasp.

Observe his *faith* in this prayer. In his confession of sin (v. 41) he discovered *repentance towards God.* In this petition He owns him to be *Lord,* and to have a *kingdom,* and that he was going to that kingdom, and that those should be happy whom he favoured; and to *believe* and *confess* all this was a *great thing* at this time of day. He believed *another life* after this, and desired to be happy in *that* life, not as the other thief, to be *saved from the cross,* but to be well provided for when the cross had done its worst.

Observe his humility in this prayer. All he begs is, *Lord remember me,* referring himself to Christ in what way to remember him. Christ remembered this thief. There is an air of importunity and fervency in this prayer. He does, as it were, breathe out his soul in it: *"Lord, remember me;* I desire no more; into thy hands I commit my case." To be remembered by Christ, now that he is in his kingdom, is what we should earnestly desire and pray for, and it will be enough to secure our welfare living and dying.

[2] The extraordinary grants of Christ's favour to him: *Jesus said unto him: "Verily I say unto thee,* I say *Amen* to this prayer: nay, thou shalt have more than thou didst ask, *This day thou shalt be with me in paradise,"* v. 43.

First, To whom this was spoken: to the penitent thief. Though Christ himself was now in the greatest struggle and agony, yet he had a word of comfort to speak to the poor penitent. Even great sinners, if they be true penitents, shall, through Christ, obtain not only the pardon of their sins, but a place in the paradise of God.

Secondly, By whom this was spoken. This was another mediatorial word which Christ spoke to explain the true intent and meaning of his sufferings; as he died to purchase the *forgiveness of sins* for us (v. 34), so also to purchase *eternal life* for us. By this word we are given to understand that Jesus Christ died to *open the kingdom of heaven to all penitent obedient believers.*

1. Christ here lets us know that he was going to paradise

himself. He went by the cross to the crown, and we must not think of going any other way. 2. He lets all penitent believers know that when they die they shall go to be with him there. See here how the happiness of heaven is set forth to us. (1) It is *paradise*, a garden of pleasure, the *paradise of God* (Rev. ii. 7). (2) It is being *with Christ* there. That is the happiness of heaven. (3) It is immediate upon death: *This day shalt thou be with me*, tonight, before tomorrow.

JUSTICE CALLED AND MERCY ANSWERED

We justly deserve the penalty of sin, but through Christ get instead His wonderful mercy. "Not by works done in righteousness, which we did in ourselves, but according to his MERCY he saved us, through the washing of REGENERATION and through renewing of the Holy Spirit" (Titus 3:5, *A.S.V.* footnote).

"Mercy glorieth against judgment" (James 2:13). Mercy overcomes the divine wrath. "Much more then, being now justified by his blood, we shall be saved from wrath through him" (Romans 5:9). "And [how you] look forward to *and* await the coming of His Son from heaven, Whom He raised from the dead, Jesus Who personally rescues *and* delivers us out of *and* from the wrath (bringing punishment) which is coming [upon the impenitent] *and* draws us to Himself [that is, invests us with all the privileges and rewards of the new life in Christ, the Messiah]" (1 Thessalonians 1:10, *Amplified New Testament*).

Christ is not any further away from us than He was from the thief on the cross. He is just a prayer away. If we call He hears us. "Then shalt thou call, and the Lord shall answer; thou shalt cry, and he shall say, Here I am" (Isaiah 58:9). "And it shall come to pass, that before they call, I will answer; and while they are yet speaking, I will hear" (Isaiah 65:24).

THE INDWELLING SPIRIT

The earliest record of filling with the Holy Spirit is that of Bezaleel (see Exodus 31:2, 3; 35:31). The Holy Spirit came upon seventy elders and they prophesied (Numbers 11:

25). The Holy Spirit entered Ezekiel (Ezekiel 2:2; 3:12, 14, 24; 8:3; 11:1, 5, 24; 31:1; 43:5). The Holy Spirit is now given to any who ask concerning such (Luke 11:13).

The Holy Spirit brought about the birth of Jesus without a human father (Matthew 1:18). John the Baptist foretold that Jesus would baptize with the Holy Spirit (Matthew 3:11). Elizabeth was filled with the Holy Spirit (Luke 1:41) as was Zacharias (Luke 1:67). The Pentecostal experience of the Holy Spirit is well known (Acts 2:1-4; 4:31). Paul received the Holy Spirit (Acts 9:17; 13:9). The Gentiles received the Holy Spirit upon their conversion (Acts 15:7, 8). Paul rebaptized "certain disciples" at Ephesus, preaching unto them the Holy Spirit, whom they received (Acts 19:1-7). We are urged to "pray in the Holy Spirit" (Jude 20). "Be filled with the Spirit" says Ephesians 5:18.

BORN AGAIN

A new heart also will I give you, and a new spirit will I put within you: and I will take away the stony heart out of your flesh, and I will give you a heart of flesh (Ezekiel 36:26).

Therefore if any man be in Christ, he is a new creature: old things are passed away; behold, all things are become new (2 Corinthians 5:17).

Being born again, not of corruptible seed, but of incorruptible, by the word of God, which liveth and abideth for ever (1 Peter 1:23).

If ye know that he is righteous, ye know that every one that doeth righteousness is born of him (1 John 2:29).

Whosoever believeth that Jesus is the Christ is born of God (1 John 5:1).

WE SUMMARIZE

The old, historic faith is expressed in what became known as "The Apostles' Creed". All who have been born of the Spirit will be open to the truths expressed herein. We quote it here in full:

I believe in God the Father Almighty, Maker of heaven and earth; and in Jesus Christ His only Son our Lord; who was conceived by the Holy Ghost, born of the virgin Mary, suffered under Pontius Pilate, was crucified, dead and buried; He descended into hell; the third day He rose again from the dead; He ascended into heaven, and sitteth at the right hand of God the Father Almighty; from thence He shall come to judge the quick and the dead. I believe in the Holy Ghost; the holy catholic church; the communion of saints; the forgiveness of sins; the resurrection of the body and the life everlasting. Amen.

The reader might well ask himself at this time whether or not he is at the moment a believer in the old, true faith.

15

Where Will You Spend Eternity?

TURNING AWAY THE UNBEGOTTEN ONES

Not all will hear the glad words, "Well done, thou good and faithful servant . . . enter thou into the joy of the Lord" (Matthew 25:21). Others will hear Him say: "Depart from me, ye cursed, into everlasting fire, prepared for the devil and his angels" (Matthew 25:41). All who are not redeemed will then hear God say, "I never knew you: depart from me, ye that work iniquity" (Matthew 7:23). As we read in Moffatt's translation of Psalm 55:15: "May they go living to the world below, swept off as their sins deserve!" "But if the Lord demonstrate by a miracle, and the earth opening its mouth, shall swallow up them and their households, and their tents, and all that belong to them; and they go down alive to the mansion of the dead; then you will know that these men have provoked the Lord" (Numbers 16:30, Thomson's *Septuagint*).

The fate of the unbegotten ones is described again at Ezekiel 32:31 (Moffatt): "The mighty warriors in the underworld shall hail him and his allies: 'Down with you, down, to a shameful death, you and all your host, amid victims of the sword!'" "For a fire is kindled in mine anger, and burneth unto the lowest Sheol" (Deuteronomy 32:22, *A.S.V.*). "I will warn you whom ye shall fear: Fear him, who after he hath killed hath authority to cast into Gehenna; yea, I say unto you, fear him" (Luke 12:5, *A.S.V.*).

The Bible is very emphatic in its description of the unbegotten ones. "You serpents! you brood of vipers! how can you escape being sentenced to Gehenna?" (Matthew 23:33, Moffatt). Such will be the fate of all those who have not been born again.

Jehovah's Witnesses simply scoff at this doctrine. Their book *Make Sure of All Things* says on page 155:

The false conception of eternal torment was introduced early into apostate Christianity, and by the fourth century after Christ was firmly entrenched in false religion. It is based on Satan's original lie in Eden.

Their *Let God Be True* book says regarding this doctrine (page 99):

The hell-fire doctrine was taught by pagans hundreds of years before Christ. It, as well as the doctrine of "purgatory",* is based on another false doctrine, that of the immortality of the human soul.

Such scoffing will end the moment the writers of the above material enter the life hereafter!

THE JUDGMENT TO COME

Hebrews 9:27 states, "It is reserved for all mankind once to die, and afterwards to be judged" (Weymouth). "It is time for the Judgment to begin with the household of God; and if it begins with us, what will be the fate of those who refuse obedience to God's gospel?" (1 Peter 4:17, Moffatt). Paul spoke of the *believers* judgment at Romans 14:10: "We shall all stand before the judgment seat of Christ", but he did not fear the judgment, for he said, "There is therefore now no condemnation to them which are in Christ Jesus ..." (Romans 8:1).

The judgment of the righteous in one thing (*bema*); the judgment of the wicked is quite another (*krisis*). Jesus Christ is the judge: "The Father judges no one; for He has given all judgment—the last judgment and the whole business of judging—entirely into the hands of the Son" (John 5:22, *Amplified New Testament*). Look at the confidence expressed by Paul, found at 2 Corinthians 5:5-10, Moffatt:

I am prepared for this change by God, who has given

*Purgatory, of course, *is* an unbiblical teaching.

me the Spirit as its pledge and instalment. Come what may, then, I am confident; I know that while I reside in the body I am away from the Lord (for I have to lead my life in faith, without seeing him): and in this confidence fain would I get away from the body and reside with the Lord. Hence also I am eager to satisfy him, whether in the body or away from it; for we have all to appear without disguise before the tribunal [*bema*] of Christ, each to be requited for what he has done with his body, well or ill.

The judgment before the great white throne is described at Revelation 20:11-15, using Moffatt's translation:

Then I saw a great white throne, and One was seated thereon; from his presence earth and sky fled, no more to be found. And before the throne I saw the dead, high and low, standing, and books were opened—also another book, the book of life, was opened—and the dead were judged by what was written in these books, by what they had done.

The sea gave up its corpses, Death and Hades gave up their dead, and all were judged by what each had done. Then Death and Hades were flung into the lake of fire, and whoever was not found enrolled in the book of Life was flung into the lake of fire—which is the second death, the lake of fire.

Compare this fate with that of the redeemed, as expressed in 1 John 2:29; 3:1, 2 (Moffatt, 1922):

As you know he is just, be sure that everyone who practices righteousness is born of him. "Born of him!" Think what a love the Father has for us, in letting us be called "children of God!" And such we are. The world does not recognize us? That is simply because it did not recognize him. We are children of God now, beloved; what we are to be is not apparent yet, but we do know that when he appears we are to be like him—for we are to see him as he is.

What a glorious certainty—to be like him! Further expressing assurance of present salvation and no fear of the judgment coming, John says at 1 John 4:13-19 (Moffatt):

This is how we may be sure we remain in him and he in us, because he has given us a share in his own Spirit; and we have seen, we do testify, that the Father has sent the Son as the Saviour of the world. Whoever confesses that "Jesus is the Son of God", in him God remains, and he remains in God; well, we do know, we have believed, the love God has for us. God is love, and he who remains in love remains in God, and God remains in him.

Love is complete with us when we have absolute confidence about the day of judgement, since in this world we are living as He lives. Love had no dread in it; no, love in its fulness drives all dread away, for dread has to do with punishment—anyone who has dread, has not reached the fulness of love. We love, because He loved us first.

Do you have this confidence?

HEAVEN OR GEHENNA—WHICH?

Eternal punishment or eternal life; two destinies—one is sure for you! Those who are righteous in Christ inherit the kingdom (Matthew 25:34); the wicked are turned away for evermore (Matthew 25:41, 46).

Eternity is a long time to regret that in this present life you made the greatest mistake a person could have made—that of rejecting Jesus Christ as God and Saviour. Once you have passed into eternity it is forever too late. *Now* is the time to receive salvation *before* it is too late.

You have only one chance to become reconciled with God, and you are living that chance now. What have you done with it? Have you made your decision yet? Why do you wait —every day it gets one day later.

LOSE YOUR FEAR IN THE MERCY OF GOD

Have no fear of men; fear rather Him whom you have rejected until now. Do not fear that by turning to Jesus Christ you could possibly do wrong. Remember, God sent His Son to redeem you, and He will show mercy toward you if you put complete faith in Christ and trust Him as your Divine Saviour. As John 17:3 reads, "And the Immortal Life is this —to know thee the one true God, and Jesus Christ whom thou hast sent as thy Messenger" (*Twentieth Century New Testament*).

You need not await the coming judgment to find out your fate as an unbeliever. John 3:18 states: "He that believeth on him is not condemned; but he that believeth not is CONDEMNED ALREADY, because he hath not believed in the name of the only begotten Son of God." Now read John 3:14, 15: "And as Moses lifted up the serpent in the wilderness, even so must the Son of man be lifted up: that whosoever believeth in him should not perish, but have eternal life." Do *more* than believe *about* Him; believe *in* Him—trust in His saving power completely.

CONSIDER THE EVERLASTING FUTURE

Consider it from the standpoint of those who have been born again, as expressed at John 10:27, 28 according to *The Amplified New Testament*:

> The sheep that are My own hear and are listening to My voice, and I know them and they follow Me, and I give them eternal life, and they shall never lose it or perish throughout the ages—to all eternity they shall never by any means be destroyed. And no one is able to snatch them out of My hand.

The formula is quite simple: "He that believeth and is baptized shall be saved; but he that disbelieveth shall be condemned" (Mark 16:16, *A.S.V.*).

THE WATCHTOWER STUMBLING-BLOCK

The Watch Tower Society has convinced Jehovah's Witnesses that they are unsaved and cannot be saved in this present life. They do not believe they will have to answer for their sins. Regarding the judgment day, *Let God Be True* says, page 283:

> There are few subjects upon which the adversary has confused and blinded the people more than upon that of the "judgment day". Many well-meaning people and sincere persons look ahead to the judgment day with a great deal

of fear and mental anguish, because of what they feel will happen to them or their loved ones when that day arrives. This, despite the fact that the Scriptures refer to it as a very joyous occasion.

The book *Make Sure of All Things* says on page 332: "Salvation to Life Involves Time and Is Not Completed When One Becomes A Christian." Compare that statement with the following Scriptures, all quoted from the *American Standard Version*:

(1) John 5:24. He that heareth my word ... HATH [present possession] eternal life, and COMETH NOT INTO JUDGMENT, but hath PASSED OUT OF DEATH INTO LIFE.

(2) 1 John 5:13. He that hath the Son HATH THE LIFE.

(3) 1 John 5:13. These things have I written ... that ye may know that YE HAVE eternal life.

(4) John 3:18. He that believeth on him is NOT JUDGED.

(5) John 3:36. He that believeth on the Son HATH ETERNAL LIFE.

(6) 1 John 2:12. I write unto you ... because your sins are FORGIVEN you.

(7) Hebrews 9:12. [Christ] entered in once for all into the holy place, having obtained ETERNAL REDEMPTION.

(8) John 10:28. I give unto them eternal life, and they shall NEVER perish.

(9) Romans 8:14, 16, 17. For as many as are led by the Spirit of God, THESE ARE THE SONS of God. The Spirit himself beareth witness with our spirit, that WE ARE CHILDREN OF GOD: AND IF CHILDREN, THEN HEIRS.

(10) Romans 8:30. Whom he foreordained, them he also called: and whom he called, them he also justified: and whom he justified, them he also glorified.

Of course, after one becomes a Christian there will be a

continuing growth in the Christian life. But the eternal life is his from the outset, and his glorification is as sure as the promises of God. There is growth *within* salvation, but not growth *into* salvation.

THE CANCELLED DEBT

The Saviour prepared a way out of love, offering you an escape. He took the penalty required by sin. It was a *substitutionary atonement*. There is now no standing debt held against the one born again, his sins are gone—cast into the sea of God's forgetfulness, to be remembered by Him no more (Jeremiah 31:34).

"While we were yet sinners, Christ died for us" (Romans 5:8). Thereby His death became death to all who accept Him as their Saviour. As we are considered dead with Christ, so we are likewise considered risen with Christ:

Knowing this, that our old man was crucified with him, that the body of sin might be done away, that we should no longer be in bondage to sin; for he that died is released from sin. But if we died with Christ, we believe that we shall also live with him. (Romans 6: 6-8, *A.S.V.*).

I have been crucified with Christ; and it is no longer I that live, but Christ liveth in me: and that life which I now live in the flesh I live in faith, the faith which is in the Son of God, who loved me, and gave himself up for me (Galatians 2:20, *A.S.V.*).

You should lose no time in coming to grips with this matter, and having your sins washed away in the blood of the Lamb. Consider what Titus 3:5-7 says:

But, when the kindness of God our Saviour and his love for man was revealed, he saved us, not as a result of any righteous actions that we had done, but in fulfilment of his merciful purposes. He saved us by that Washing which was a New Birth to us, and by the renewing power of the Holy Spirit, which he poured out upon us abundantly through Jesus Christ our Saviour; that, having been pronounced righteous through his loving-kindness, we might enter on

215

our inheritance with the hope of Immortal Life. (*Twentieth Century New Testament*.)

WORKS FOLLOWING SALVATION

My beloved, you have always been obedient, not only when I have been with you but even more so when I have been absent. So now you must demonstrate your own salvation with fear and trembling. It is really God who works in you, so that you are not only willing but also able to carry out His loving purposes (Philippians 2:12, Norlie).

Consider the above words from *Living Letters, The Paraphrased Epistles* by Kenneth N. Taylor (published by the Billy Graham Evangelistic Association, Minneapolis):

Dearest friends, when I was there with you, you were always so careful to follow my instructions. And now that I am away you must be even more careful to do the good things that result from being saved, obeying God with deep reverence, shrinking back from all that might displease Him.

It is only fitting and proper to assume that good works will follow a person's having obtained salvation. God's will through you can be expressed in works. Faith is unseen to man; only proper works can demonstrate the unseen faith within. But these works add nothing to one's salvation. Salvation cannot be added to by one's works. Christ did not give us a salvation short of completion. But our works can show how great and complete a salvation we have received and what it has done to change us. " 'Then what must we do', they asked, 'if we are to work as God would have us work?' Jesus replied, 'This is the work that God requires: believe in the one whom he has sent!" (John 6:29, *New English Bible*). Never let the works of such groups as Jehovah's Witnesses fool you into thinking they are God's people. "No one who disowns the Son can possess the Father: HE WHO CONFESSES THE SON POSSESSES THE FATHER AS WELL" (1 John 2:23, Moffatt). Determine those with whom you shall fellowship thus:

Do not believe every spirit, beloved, but test the spirits to see if they come from God; for many false prophets have emerged in the world. You can recognize the Spirit of God by this: every spirit which confesses Jesus as the Christ incarnate comes from God, and any spirit who does not confess Jesus incarnate does not come from God. This latter is the spirit of antichrist; you were told it was coming, and here it is already in the world. (1 John 4:1-4, Moffatt, 1922.)

THE EVANGELICAL FAITH

All of Christendom does not preach the redemptive gospel. Many elements within these ranks teach a most damnable heresy. There are some clergymen who teach as much heresy as does the Watch Tower Society. After you have been born again you want to be careful with whom you fellowship. Watch out for those who deny the deity of Christ and other fundamental doctrines of Christianity.

The various denominations differ over such matters as mode of baptism, form of church government, dispensationalism, etc. However, if they preach the blood of Christ, the other matters are to be considered secondary. Satisfy *yourself* as to where you choose to stand on these various matters. Men are not saved as a result of hearing a dispute between those who advocate the ecumenical movement and the separatists.

These disputes will still be going on when you and I are dead and gone! It is this writer's opinion that preaching the gospel without causing dissension among the brethren is to be preferred.

You become a member of the body of Christ (and hence, the Church) through being born again; thus you are born into the family of God—the eternal family. You will learn to love the saints of God and work along with them in preaching Christ and Him crucified.

THE BEAUTIFUL CITY

John was privileged beyond other apostles in that he saw in vision the heavenly city. His description is as follows, quoting first from Revelation 21:21-26, Weymouth:

The twelve gates were twelve pearls; each of them consisting of a single pearl. And the main street of the city was made of pure gold, resembling transparent glass. I saw no temple in the city, for the Lord God, the Ruler of all, is its temple, and so is the Lamb. Nor has the city any need of the sun or of the moon, to give it light; for the glory of God has illumined it and its lamp is the Lamb. By its light the nations will walk; and into it the kings of the earth are to bring their glory. And in the daytime (for there will be no night there) the gates will never be closed.

Continuing on, we read the following from chapter 22, verses 1-5:

Then he showed me the river of the Water of Life, bright as crystal, issuing from the throne of God and of the Lamb. On either side of the river, midway between it and the main street of the city, was the Tree of Life. It produced twelve kinds of fruit, yielding a fresh crop month by month, and the leaves of the trees served as medicine for the nations.

"Nothing accursed will be there," he said; "but the throne of God and of the Lamb will be in that city. And His servants will render Him holy service and will see His face, and His name will be on their foreheads. And there will be no night there; and they have no need of lamplight or sunlight, for the Lord God will illumine them, and they will be kings for ever and ever."

Reading now chapter 22, verses 14 and 15 from Moffatt's 1922 translation:

Blessed are they who wash their robes, that theirs may be the right to the tree of Life, the right to enter the gates of the City. Begone, you dogs, you sorcerers, you vicious creatures, you murderers, you idolaters, you who love and practice falsehood, every one of you!

Moffatt's translation contains verses 16, 13, 12 and 17 in that order:

"I Jesus have sent my angel to give you this testimony for the churches; I am the Scion and offspring of David, the bright star of the morning. I am the alpha and the omega, the First and the Last, the beginning and the end. Lo, I am coming very soon, with my reward, to requite everyone for what he has done." "Come," say the Spirit and the Bride: let the hearer too say, "Come"; and let the thirsty come, let anyone who desires it, take the water of Life without price.

Take note of these words from Revelation 1:7, 8 (Moffatt):

Lo, he is coming on the clouds, to be seen by every eye, even by those who impaled him, and all the tribes of earth shall wail because of him: even so, Amen. "I am the alpha and the omega," saith the Lord God, who is and who was and is coming, the almighty.

Reading now verses 12, 13, 17 and 18 from the same translation:

I turned to see whose voice it was that spoke to me; and on turning round I saw seven golden lampstands and in the middle of the lampstands One who resembled a human being ... When I saw him, I fell at his feet like a dead man; but he laid his hand on me, saying, "Be not afraid; I am the First and the Last, I was dead and here I am alive for evermore, holding the keys that unlock death and Hades."

This holy city will be the eternal dwelling-place of all who have been redeemed. Will you meet us in the city? Or will we search heaven never to find you there?

THE FINAL CALL

Let not your heart be troubled: Believe in God, believe also in me. In my Father's house are many abodes; were it not so, would I have told you that I go prepare you a place? And when I go and prepare you a place, I am coming again and I will welcome you to my home, that where I am, you may be also (John 14:1-3, Moffatt, 1901).

Lay aside those garments that are stained with sin
And be washed in the blood of the Lamb;
There's a fountain flowing for the soul unclean,
O be washed in the blood of the Lamb!

219

There is a fountain filled with blood,
Drawn from Emmanuel's veins;
And sinners, plunged beneath that flood,
Lose all their guilty stains.

Dear dying Lamb, Thy precious blood
Will never lose its power,
Till all the ransomed church of God
Be saved, to sin no more.

You will be welcome in the holy city, if you accept the invitation now. "Blessed are they that wash their robes, that they may have the right to come to the tree of life, and may enter in by the gates of the city" (Revelation 22:14, *A.S.V.*).

TO THE CHRISTIANS

I cannot close this book without giving you some suggestions on how to witness to Jehovah's Witnesses when they come to your door. It may be that the Lord will use you to lead some of them to the Saviour. Here is what I suggest:

(1) Do not permit the J. W. to give his message—YOU take the initiative.
   a. Thank him for calling
   b. Commend his interest in the Bible
   c. You might say: "I'm glad the Lord sent you here to see me!"

(2) Identify yourself as a *Christian*, rather than by denominational affiliation; many Witnesses have never seen the inside of a church!

(3) Give in full your testimony as to how you became a Christian.
   a. Describe the new birth, giving Scriptures as opportunity affords.
   b. Be certain to make plain that what Christ has done for others He will do for the J. W.—*if* he accepts Christ as his Saviour.

(4) Following your testimony hand the J. W. gospel tracts or other literature.

    a. Ask him to read it with his Bible upon returning home.

    b. If he offers *you* some literature, do not pay for it; however, you might exchange your literature for his.

    c. Be careful the literature you receive does not come into the hands of any unsaved persons in your house.

(5) Dismiss the J. W. politely; here is what you might do:

    Say: "In our church, we believe in praying for *others*, and we would like to be praying for you! *My* name is ... ; what is *yours*?

(6) Put that name on your prayer list and be praying for that Witness.

(7) IF *two* of them approach you, *one* of them is not a J. W., but is a trainee!

    a. Cut them off, saying: "I have to ask you a question!" When they have become quiet, inquire: "Which one of you is training the other?"

    b. One of them should identify himself: "*I'm* being trained!"

    c. Ignore the other one and proceed to witness to *him*, as outlined above!

(8) If you can obtain the name of the trainee, it might be well for someone in the church qualified for this work to follow up, and call on that family—snatching them like a brand from the burning away from the Kingdom Hall!

IN FINALITY

Our hope is so grand and glorious, the following poem barely does it justice:

> There's no disappointment in Heaven
> No weariness, sorrow or pain;
> No hearts that are bleeding and broken,
> No song with a minor refrain.

The clouds of our earthly horizon
Will never appear in the sky,
For all will be sunshine and gladness
With never a sob nor a sigh.

We'll never pay rent for our mansion,
The taxes will never come due;
Our garments will never grow threadbare,
But always be fadeless and new.
We'll never grow hungry nor thirsty,
Nor languish in poverty there,
For all the rich bounties of Heaven
His sanctified children will share.

There'll never be crepe on the door-knob
No funeral train in the sky;
No graves on the hillsides of Glory,
For there we shall nevermore die.
The old will be young there forever,
Transformed in a moment of time;
Immortal we'll stand in His likeness,
The stars and the sun to outshine.

I'm bound for that beautiful city
My Lord has prepared for His own;
Where all the redeemed of all ages
Sing "Glory!" around the white throne;
Sometimes I grow homesick for Heaven,
And the glories I there shall behold:
What a joy that will be when my Saviour I see,
In that beautiful City of gold!

F. M. Lehman

(From *Poems That Preach*, Zondervan Publishing House, 1952).

Throughout the period of time I have been separated from the Watchtower movement, many Witnesses have spread lies about me, in order to make it evident to all that I was disfellowshipped from the Society for some impropriety. The Watchtower Society itself had better sense than to put this in writing; one would assume the Witnesses would, also! However, this letter is evidence to the contrary:

> *If you ever come this way I will attend your meeting and after your talk I will speak in presence of all that you were disfellowshipped by Watch Tower Society because you practiced immorality.*

If the writer is shocked to find this appearing in print, let me remind her that she can be considered fortunate that I did not proceed with legal action!

Note how her letter and that from the Kingdom Hall contradict each other. Which one is true? Then the other is a lie! Let the Witnesses now decide! And if the letter from this woman is a lie, then let them consider how they themselves were victims of their own lies all these years!

I call upon all Jehovah's Witnesses who have been made a victim of the Watchtower Society's lies to quit any further activity with the organization and immediately begin to seek the face of Jesus Christ and be saved. Know this for certain: Any who seek Him will never be turned away. There was never one who sought his Saviour who was disappointed. See John 6:37.

Look at this contradiction!

This statement appears in *Let God Be True*, page 107:

> A little searching of any Greek-English dictionary will reveal that the Greek word *pneuma* translated "spirit" is the SAME WORD translated also in the Bible as "wind" (Emphasis mine).

Now note the following from *Aid to Bible Understanding* (1971 edition), from page 1658:

> Although at John 3:8 *pneuma* (generally translated "spirit") means "wind," the Greek term *anemos* is the more frequently used designation for wind. . . .

On the Deity of Jesus Christ, please consider the following:
In Bagster's edition of the *Septuagint* we find the following
expression at Deuteronomy 32:39: IDETE IDETE HOTI
EGO EIMI, KAI OUK ESTI THEOS PLEN EMOU. He
translates this as follows: *Behold, behold that I am, and
there is no god beside me.* The God with whom there is no
other god calls Himself EGO EIMI. No Jehovah's Witness
dare deny that this is Jehovah God Himself. Compare this
with the words of Christ at John 8:58: PRIN ABRAHAM
GENESTHAI EGO EIMI. Christ here says, *Before Abraham
was,* EGO EIMI. Jehovah and Jesus are *both* EGO EIMI in
the Bible.

Using the *New World* Bible, compare the words of Hebrews
1:10-12 which clearly apply to Jesus, with Psalms 102:24-26,
which words apply to God. The passage in Hebrews is a quote
from the Psalms. In Psalms the passage applies to Jehovah
God and in Hebrews to Jesus Christ.

Note particularly the following: In the pasage at Revelation 22:12-16, the quotation marks are strictly those of the
translator. No quotation marks occur in the Greek manscripts.
Therefore, quotation marks are not part of the inspired
Scriptures. Read this passage without use of the quotation
marks and note *the Alpha and Omega* (who is Jehovah God
at Rev. 1:8), is *the first and the last* (which, according to the
edition with marginal references is Jehovah at Isaiah 48:12)
who is Jesus at Rev. 1:17, 18, and *says* He is Jesus at 22:16.

Note also: The One who says He is coming at 22:12 is
Jesus in verse 20.

All interested persons may write:

Rev. Ted Dencher
Post Office Box 199
Sharon, Pa. 16146, USA